≫*Twenty Letters to a Friend*

Svetlana Alliluyeva

Twenty Letters to a Friend

Translated by Priscilla Johnson McMillan

Harper & Row, Publishers | New York and Evanston

Library of Congress Catalog Card Number: 67-26472

Designed by The Etheredges

→→→ To My Mother

⫸ Author's Note

These letters were written during the summer of 1963 in the village of Zhukovka, outside Moscow. The writing took thirty-five days. The free letter form enabled me to be completely candid. I believe that I am, in a way, bearing witness.

It did not occur to me at the time that the book I was writing might be published.

Now that I am able to publish it, I have left it just as it was although it is four years later and I am far from Russia. Apart from necessary corrections, nonsubstantive cuts and the addition of footnotes while I was preparing the manuscript for publication, the book remains as it was when it was read by my friends in Moscow. I should like the reader of these letters to feel that they were written to him.

SVETLANA ALLILUYEVA

Locust Valley, New York
May, 1967

➤➤Twenty Letters to a Friend

➤➤➤ *Introduction*

July 16, 1963

It's quiet here. Moscow, breathing fire like a human volcano with its smoldering lava of passion, ambition and politics, its hurly-burly of meetings and entertainment, Moscow is less than twenty miles away. There is a World Congress of Women, a World Film Festival, talks with China and news from all over the world morning, noon and night. Some visitors from Hungary have arrived. Movie actors from everywhere in the world are exploring the city. African women are buying souvenirs at GUM.[1]* Red Square is full of men and women of all races. Each one has brought a singular destiny of his own, his own character and soul.

Moscow seethes and bubbles and gasps for air. It's always thirsting for something new, the newest events, the latest sensation. Everyone wants to be the first to know. It's the rhythm of life today.

[* Superior numbers refer to Translator's Notes, beginning on p. 237.]

Here, it is quiet.

Evening sun lights the grass and the woods with gold. These woods are a small oasis between Odintsovo, Barvikha and Romashkovo, an oasis where roads and *dachas* aren't built any more, where the woods have been cleared, the grass is mowed in the clearings and the underbrush cut away. People come here from Moscow to relax. On radio and television they keep saying the best way to relax on your day off is to hike with a knapsack and walking stick from Odintsovo to Usovo or Ilyin-skoye, to walk the paths through our splendid forest across ravines and clearings and groves of birch. The visitor from Moscow has only to spend three or four hours roaming the forest and breathing its air to feel cured, strengthened, reborn, rested from all his cares. He puts a faded bouquet of wild-flowers onto the rack of the electric train and goes back to the teeming streets of Moscow. For a long time after that he'll ad-vise everyone he knows to spend Sunday hiking in the woods. Sooner or later they'll all go by on the path, past my fence and the house I live in.

I've lived in these woods and this part of the world all my thirty-seven years. What difference does it make that my life and these houses have changed? The woods are still the same. Usovo is in the same place, and the village of Kolchuga and the hill above it from which you can see in every direction. The villages are the same, too. The villagers still draw their water from wells and do their cooking on kerosene stoves. Cows still low and hens cluck inside the village huts. Yet tele-vision antennas stick up from the gray, tumbledown roofs, and the girls wear nylon blouses and sandals from Hungary. A good deal is changing even here, but the grass and the birch forest have the same sweet smell as you get off the train, the golden pines are just the same and the same country roads go off to Petrovskoye and Znamenskoye. This is my home.

This is where I belong—not in the city or the Kremlin, which I cannot stand and where I lived for twenty-five years. And when I die, let them bury me in the ground here in Romashkovo, in the graveyard by the station, on the little hill. There's a feeling of space there; there are fields and sky. There's a nice old church on the hill. True, it's not used any more and it's falling down and the trees have grown up rank in the enclosure around it, but it stands splendid in the dense greenery and goes on all the same serving the cause of everlasting good on earth. Let them bury me there. I don't want to be in the city for anything. I would suffocate there.

I'm telling you this, my friend, so that you shall know. You want to know all about me. Then you should know this, too.

You say you want to know everything about me and the life I led, everything I knew and saw around me. A lot of it was interesting, of course. But what happened isn't nearly so important as what one thinks about it now. Would you like to join me as I think?

I shall write you about everything. The one good thing about not seeing you is that I can write you letters. I shall not see you for five weeks, my friend, who understand and want to know everything.

This will be one long letter to you. You'll find all kinds of things here—portraits, sketches, life stories, love, nature, well-known events both great and small, my own thoughts about them, the remarks and opinions of friends and everybody else I knew. It will be a varied, untidy tale and it will all pour out unexpectedly, for this is what my life was like.

Please don't think I look on my life as anything special. On the contrary, the life I've led has been unusually dull and monotonous for one of my generation. Maybe it hasn't even begun yet. Maybe when I've written it all down, an unbearable burden of some kind will fall from my shoulders at last and then my real life will begin. I'm secretly counting on this. It's the hope I cherish in my heart. I've grown so weary of this weight. Maybe I shall be able to throw it off at last.

Most of my generation have had much fuller lives than I, particularly the ones who are five or six years older. They're the ones who went fearlessly and eagerly straight from their classrooms to the war. Few of them survived. Those who did are the flower of our time. They are the Decembrists of tomorrow —they will yet teach all of us how we must live. They will have their say, of this I am certain. Russia is so hungry for a word of wisdom and longs for new words and deeds.

I shall never catch up with them. I have no great deeds to my credit; I've never been an actor on center stage. All my life was spent behind the scenes. But, you ask, isn't it interesting there, too?

It's dark behind the scenes. You can see the audience applauding, open-mouthed with delight, following the speeches and blinded by the multicolored lights and the scenery. You can see the actors, too, playing their roles as Czars, gods, servants and extras. You can see whether they're acting or whether they're talking with one another naturally. There's a smell of mice and glue and old sets. But what an interesting place it is to watch! It's where the makeup men, the prompters and the costume people have their being. They wouldn't change their lives for anything. No one knows better than they that all of life is an enormous theater where by no means everyone is cast in the role he was meant for. The play goes on, passions boil, the heroes brandish their swords, poets recite, Czars are crowned, castles on the stage tumble and spring up again in the twinkling of an eye, Yaroslavna[2] weeps for Igor on the fortress wall, the fairies and evil spirits fly, the ghost of the King appears, Hamlet broods—and the people are silent.[3]

My story will be a long one and these letters will be long. I shall get out of sequence and go back to the very beginning. God forbid that you should think of this as a novel, a biography or a memoir, or a consecutive story of any kind.

This is such a wonderful morning, a forest morning. Birds are singing and sunlight is filtering through the green half-darkness of the forest. I shall tell you today about the very end, the days in early March, 1953, when I was in my father's house watching as he lay dying. Was this really the end of one era and the beginning of another, as people are saying now? It's not for me to judge—we shall have to wait and see. My subject is not an era, but people.

They were terrible days. The feeling that the steady, firm and familiar ground was swaying beneath my feet began on

March 2, when I was called out of French class at the Academy and told that "Malenkov[1] wants you to come to Blizhny." (Blizhny, the Russian word for "near," was the name of my father's *dacha* at Kuntsevo, just outside Moscow, to distinguish it from his other houses, which were farther away.) It was unprecedented for anyone but my father to ask me to come to the *dacha*. I went with a strange feeling of disquiet.

When we were through the gates and Khrushchev[2] and Bulganin[3] waved my car to a stop in the drive outside the house, I thought it must be all over. They took me by the arms as I got out. They were both in tears. "Let's go in," they said. "Beria[4] and Malenkov will tell you everything."

Even in the front hall, nothing was the same as usual. Instead of the customary deep silence, everyone was bustling and running around. When someone finally told me that my father had had a stroke in the night and was unconscious, I even felt a little relieved. I had thought he was already dead. They'd found him at three in the morning, in the room I was standing in, right there, lying on a rug by the sofa. They decided to carry him to the next room, to the sofa he usually slept on. That's where he was now. The doctors were in there, too. "You can go in," somebody told me.

I listened in a haze. The details no longer had any meaning. I could take in only one thing: he was dying. I hadn't yet talked to the doctors, but I didn't doubt it for a second. It was plain that this whole house and everything around me were already dying under my very eyes. The whole three days I was there, I saw only this one thing. It was obvious there couldn't be any other outcome.

There was a great crowd of people jammed into the big room where my father was lying. Doctors I didn't know, who were seeing him for the first time—Academician V. N. Vinogradov,[5] who'd looked after my father for many years, was

now in jail—were making a tremendous fuss, applying leeches
to his neck and the back of his head, making cardiograms and
taking X-rays of his lungs. A nurse kept giving him injections
and a doctor jotted it all down in a notebook. Everything
was being done as it should be.

Everyone was rushing around trying to save a life that
could no longer be saved. A special session of the Academy of
Medical Sciences was being held somewhere to decide what
further steps should be taken. Another group of doctors was
conferring in the next room. An artificial-respiration machine
had been brought from one of the medical research institutes.
Some young doctors had come with it, since no one else had
the faintest idea how to work it. The unwieldy thing was just
standing there idle, and the young doctors were staring dis-
tractedly around, utterly overcome by what was going on.
Suddenly I realized that I knew that young woman doctor over
there and wondered where I'd seen her before. We nodded but
didn't say anything. Everyone was tiptoeing around as quiet
as a mouse. They all felt that something portentous, something
almost of majesty, was going on in this room and they conducted themselves accordingly.

There was only one person who was behaving in a way that
was very nearly obscene. That was Beria. He was extremely
agitated. His face, repulsive enough at the best of times, now
was twisted by his passions—by ambition, cruelty, cunning and
a lust for power and more power still. He was trying so hard
at this moment of crisis to strike exactly the right balance, to
be cunning, yet not too cunning. It was written all over him.
He went up to the bed and spent a long time gazing into the
dying man's face. From time to time my father opened his eyes
but was apparently unconscious or in a state of semiconscious-
ness. Beria stared fixedly at those clouded eyes, anxious even
now to convince my father that he was the most loyal and

devoted of them all, as he had always tried with every ounce of his strength to appear to be. Unfortunately, he had succeeded for too long.

During the final minutes, as the end was approaching, Beria suddenly caught sight of me and ordered: "Take Svetlana away!" Those who were standing nearby stared, but no one moved. Afterward he darted into the hallway ahead of anybody else. The silence of the room where everyone was gathered around the deathbed was shattered by the sound of his loud voice, the ring of triumph unconcealed, as he shouted, "Khrustalyov![6] My car!"

He was a magnificent modern specimen of the artful courtier, the embodiment of Oriental perfidy, flattery and hypocrisy who had succeeded in confounding even my father, a man whom it was ordinarily difficult to deceive. A good deal that this monster did is now a blot on my father's name, and in a good many things they were guilty together. But I haven't the slightest doubt that Beria used his cunning to trick my father into many other things and laughed up his sleeve about it afterwards. All the other leaders knew it.

Now all the ugliness inside him came into the open—he couldn't hold it back. I was by no means the only one to see it. But they were all terrified of him. They knew that the moment my father died no one in all of Russia would have greater power in his grasp.

My father was lying there unconscious. The stroke had been severe. He'd lost his speech, and his right side was paralyzed. He opened his eyes several times, but his gaze was clouded and no one knew whether he recognized anybody or not. Whenever he opened his eyes they leaned over him, straining to catch a word or even read a wish in his eyes. I was sitting at his side holding his hand and he looked at me, though I'm sure he couldn't see me. I kissed his face and his hand. There was no longer anything more for me to do.

It's a strange thing, but during those days of illness when he was nothing but a body out of which the soul had flown and later, during the days of leavetaking in the Hall of Columns,[7] I loved my father more tenderly than I ever had before. He'd been very remote from me, from us, his children, and all his relatives. During the past few years enormous blown-up photographs of children, a little boy on skis, a boy in a blossoming cherry tree, had appeared in his rooms at the *dacha*, but he hadn't once found time to see five of his eight grandchildren. Yet even the grandchildren who never saw him loved him—and love him still. During those days, when he found peace at last on his deathbed and his face became beautiful and serene, I felt my heart breaking from grief and love.

Neither before nor since have I felt such a powerful welling up of strong, contradictory emotions. As I stood in the Hall of Columns day after day, frozen and unable to speak (I literally stood, for try as they would to make me sit down and even though they shoved a chair under me, I was unable to sit or do anything but stand in the presence of what was occurring), I realized that a deliverance of some kind was under way. I had no idea what kind of deliverance it was or what form it was going to take, but I knew that for me and for everyone else it would be a release from a burden that had been weighing on the minds and hearts of us all. They were playing an old Georgian folk tune with a melody that was sorrowful and full of feeling. I looked at that beautiful face in its sadness and repose and listened to the funeral music and felt torn apart by grief. I thought what a bad daughter I had been, that I'd been more like a stranger than a daughter, and had never been a help to this lonely spirit, this sick old man, when he was left all alone on his Olympus. Yet he was, after all, my father, a father who had done his best to love me and to whom

I owed good things as well as bad. All those days I couldn't cry and I didn't eat. Grief and a sort of calm had turned me to stone.

My father died a difficult and terrible death. It was the first and so far the only time I have seen somebody die. God grants an easy death only to the just.

The hemorrhaging had gradually spread to the rest of the brain. Since his heart was healthy and strong, it affected the breathing centers bit by bit and caused suffocation. His breathing became shorter and shorter. For the last twelve hours the lack of oxygen was acute. His face altered and became dark. His lips turned black and the features grew unrecognizable. The last hours were nothing but a slow strangulation. The death agony was horrible. He literally choked to death as we watched. At what seemed like the very last moment he suddenly opened his eyes and cast a glance over everyone in the room. It was a terrible glance, insane or perhaps angry and full of the fear of death and the unfamiliar faces of the doctors bent over him. The glance swept over everyone in a second. Then something incomprehensible and awesome happened that to this day I can't forget and don't understand. He suddenly lifted his left hand as though he were pointing to something above and bringing down a curse on us all. The gesture was incomprehensible and full of menace, and no one could say to whom or at what it might be directed. The next moment, after a final effort, the spirit wrenched itself free of the flesh.

I thought I was about to suffocate, too, and I clutched the hand of a young woman doctor who was standing next to me. She started moaning from pain, and we held on tightly to one another.

The spirit had flown. The flesh grew still. The face became pale and assumed its usual appearance. In a few seconds it was serene, beautiful, imperturbable. We all stood frozen and silent for a few minutes. I've no idea for how long, but it seemed like ages.

The members of the government then rushed for the door. They had to go to Moscow, to the Central Committee building, where everyone was sitting and waiting for the news. They went with the information everyone was secretly expecting. To be fair, they were torn by the same contradictory emotions as I—by sorrow and relief.

All of them except the utterly degenerate Beria spent those days in great agitation, trying to help yet at the same time fearful of what the future might bring. Many of them shed genuine tears. I saw Voroshilov,[8] Kaganovich,[9] Malenkov, Bulganin and Khrushchev in tears. The fact is that, besides being bound to him by a common cause, they were under the spell of his extraordinary personality, which carried people away and was utterly impossible to resist. Many people knew this through their own experience—of these, some admit it, though others now deny it.

Finally everyone had gone. The body lay on its deathbed and according to custom was to lie there for several hours more. Bulganin and Mikoyan[10] stayed behind. I stayed, too, and sat on a sofa by the opposite wall. The doctors went home and half the lights were put out. The only other person left was an old nurse whom I'd seen around the Kremlin hospital for years. She was quietly tidying up the large dining table in the center of the room.

This was the room where everyone ate and where the tiny circle of the Politburo used to hold its meetings. Affairs of state had been discussed and settled at this table over supper and dinner. Coming to "dinner" at my father's always meant coming to decide some question or other. There was an enormous rug on the floor. Along the walls there were sofas and chairs and in the corner a fireplace. My father always liked a fire in winter. In one of the corners there was a record player. My father had a good collection of Russian, Georgian and Ukrainian folk songs and didn't recognize the existence of any other kind of music. He'd spent all his last years, nearly twenty of them, in this room and now it was saying good-bye to its master.

My father's servants and bodyguards came to say good-bye. They felt genuine grief and emotion. Cooks, chauffeurs and watchmen, gardeners and the women who had waited on the table, all came quietly in. They went up to the bed silently and wept. They wiped their tears away as children do, with their hands and sleeves and kerchiefs. Many were sobbing. The nurse, who was also in tears, gave them drops of valerian. I looked on, quite numb, sitting or standing, and my eyes were completely dry. I couldn't leave. I just watched and watched, unable to tear myself away.

Valentina Istomina, or "Valechka," as she was called, who had been my father's housekeeper for eighteen years, came in to say good-bye. She dropped heavily to her knees, put her head on my father's chest and wailed at the top of her voice as the women in villages do. She went on for a long time and nobody tried to stop her.

All these men and women who were servants of my father loved him. In little things he wasn't hard to please. On the contrary, he was courteous, unassuming and direct with those who waited on him. He never scolded anyone except the top men, the generals and commandants of his bodyguard. The servants had neither bullying nor harshness to complain of. They often asked him for help, in fact, and no one was ever refused. During his last years Valechka and all the rest of them had known more about him and had seen more of him than I, who no longer felt close to him and was living in a different place. She had seen people from all over the world at that large table during the banquets at which she always served. She had seen a good deal that was interesting, within her own narrow limits, of course, and whenever I see her now she tells me about it in the most vivid and amusing way. Like everyone who worked for my father she'll be convinced to her dying day that no better man ever walked the earth. Nothing will ever make them change their minds.

Late that night, or, rather, when it was nearly daybreak, they came to take the body for the autopsy. I started shaking all over with a nervous trembling of some kind. I couldn't cry. I just trembled all over. The body was laid on a stretcher. It was the first time I had seen my father naked. It was a beautiful body. It didn't look old or as if he'd been sick at all. With a pang like the thrust of a knife in the heart I felt what it meant to be "flesh of the flesh." I realized that the body that had given me life no longer had life or breath in it, yet I would go on living.

You can never understand what this means until you've witnessed the death of a parent. To understand death you have to see it with your own eyes. You have to watch as the "spirit departs the flesh," leaving only the mortal remains. It wasn't so much that I understood this at the time as that I sensed it. The knowledge of it passed across my heart and left a mark.

The body was taken away. A white car was driven up to the doorway and everyone came outside. Those who were standing on the porch or in the driveway took off their hats. I was still trembling all over. Someone put a coat over my shoulders as I stood in the doorway. Bulganin put his arms around me. The doors slammed shut and the car started up. I buried my face in Bulganin's chest and finally started to cry. He cried, too, and stroked my hair. The others lingered a little longer in the doorway and then started to drift away.

I went to the servants' wing, which was connected to the

house by a long passageway that was used for bringing food
from the kitchen. Everyone who was left, the nurses, bodyguards and servants, had gathered there. We sat in the servants' dining room, a big room with a radio and a serving
counter. Over and over again they talked about how it all had
happened. Somebody made me eat. "You're going to have a
long day," they told me. "You haven't had any sleep and you're
going to the Hall of Columns soon. You'd better get your
strength up!" I had something to eat and sat for a while in an
armchair. It was five in the morning. I went into the kitchen.
On the way I heard someone sobbing loudly. The nurse who'd
been developing cardiograms in the bathroom was crying as
if her heart would break. "Just look at that. She locked herself
in and has been crying for hours," somebody told me.

As we sat in the dining room, all of us were unconsciously
waiting for the same thing. At six in the morning the radio
would announce the news we already knew. But everyone
needed to *hear* it. It was as if we couldn't believe it otherwise.
Finally it was six o'clock. A voice came on, the slow voice of
Levitan,[11] or someone who sounded like Levitan, a voice associated with announcements of major importance. Then, at
last, we took it in. Men, women, everyone, started crying all
over again. I broke down and wept and felt better because I
wasn't alone, because all these people knew what an immense
thing it was that had happened and were weeping with me.

All of them were sincere. No one was making a show of
loyalty or grief. All of them had known one another for years.
All of them knew me, too. They knew that I had been a bad
daughter and that my father had been a bad father, but that he
had loved me all the same, as I loved him.

No one in this room looked on him as a god or a superman,
a genius or a demon. They loved and respected him for the
most ordinary human qualities, those qualities of which servants are the best judges of all.

→» *2*

Why did I write you about this today? Why did I want to begin
with this?

It's ten years since then, quite a long time for our hectic,
supersonic age. Since then, I haven't been back once to the
gloomy *dacha* at Kuntsevo and I no longer go to the Kremlin.
There's nothing to draw me to either place. My father never
cared about possessions. He led a puritanical life, and the
things that belonged to him said very little about him. The
ones he left behind—his house, his rooms and his apartment—
give no clue to what he was like.

The only places I enjoy thinking back on are the ones I lived
in with my mother: the apartment we had in the Kremlin up
to 1932, and Zubalovo, our *dacha* near Usovo. You could feel
my mother's presence in both of them. I shall tell you about
this later.

Ten years have gone by. My life has changed very little. I live, as I always did, in my father's shadow. As before, my children and I still have a comparatively secure life. As before, the attention of some, the dislike of others and the curiosity of absolutely everyone, disappointments and upsets whether deserved or not, to say nothing of the many expressions of loyalty and love that I do not deserve—all these things continue to weigh on me and hem me in on all sides as they did while my father was alive. I can't break out of these confines.

He is gone, but his shadow still stands over all of us. It still dictates to us and we, very often, obey.

Meanwhile, life is in ferment all around us. An entire generation has grown up to whom neither the name of Stalin nor a great deal else, both good and bad, that is associated with his name means anything at all. This generation will usher in a life of which we know nothing. We shall see what it turns out to be like. People want to be happy. They want bright colors, fireworks, noise, excitement. They also want culture and knowledge. They want the way of life the rest of Europe has enjoyed for so long to come to Russia at last. They want to speak all languages and visit every country on earth. They are hungry for all these things and can hardly wait for them. They want comfort, smart clothing and decent furniture, not village homespun and clumsy, old-fashioned things. They eagerly adopt everything from abroad—dress, hair styles, ideas, art, the latest trends in philosophy—and relentlessly discard our own achievements and our own Russian traditions. And who can condemn them? It's natural enough, after all, after so many years of austerity and living in puritanical style, of being walled off from the rest of the world.

It's not for me to condemn. I don't particularly like abstract art, for instance, but I can see why it appeals not just to half-educated adolescents but to people who are anything but stupid. It isn't for me to argue with them. They have a keener sense of the present and future than I do. Why should anyone try to keep them from thinking as they please?

There's no danger in all these harmless enthusiasms. The danger lies in a know-nothing, Philistine attitude, in not caring about anything, old or new, foreign or domestic. The danger lies in ignorance and the complacent assumption that in our time everything has already been achieved and that if the production of pig iron, eggs and milk can be raised, then the paradise dreamed of by a benighted humanity will truly have come into being.

Forgive me if I stray from the point. I was thinking about the fact that my life hasn't changed much during the past ten years. I spend all my time thinking over what's happened and trying to make sense of it all. It's the kind of thing that can drive you out of your mind. Isn't this what poor Hamlet did and didn't he despise himself for it?

My weird and preposterous double life goes on as before. I'm still living, as I did ten years ago, an outer life that is one thing and an inner life that is something quite else again. My outer life is secure and I live as before, somewhere on the fringe of the government elite, enjoying the same material privileges. My inner life, on the other hand, is one of total alienation from all these people, from their customs and interests, their spirit and deeds, and it is an alienation I feel even more strongly than ever. When I tell you how my life took shape, you'll see that it had to be this way, both before and now.

I'm not the kind who can write about what I don't know and haven't seen with my own eyes. I'm not a professional writer. I'd never attempt to write a biography of my father, which, after all, would have to cover twenty years of the last century and half of this one. I can only judge what I saw and experienced myself or what is at least within the limits of my own

understanding. I can write about the twenty-seven years that I
spent with my father, about the people who came to his house
or were close to him, about everything that was around us and
made up our life, about the various individuals and their conflicting efforts to shape it, and maybe I can write about other
things, too. All this covered only a small part, about a third, of
my father's life, and an even smaller part, perhaps just a micro-
scopic fraction, of life in general. But all of life must be looked
at through a microscope. We've become too accustomed to
making over-all judgments. Isn't this, after all, the root of all
our superficial intolerance and dogmatism?

The life of the tiny cross-section of society that was my family was, as a Soviet literary critic might put it, typical.

The twentieth century and the Revolution turned everything upside down. Wealth and poverty, pauper and aristo-
crat all changed places. Yet with all the reshuffling and the
dislocation, all the impoverishment and redistribution of
wealth, Russia was still Russia, still a country that had to go on
living and building itself up and moving forward, trying to
assimilate new things, keep up with the rest of the world, catch
up and even move ahead.

Maybe in the midst of so much turmoil there is something
of interest to be found in family chronicles, in the portraits
of people who were close to us but unknown to the world outside. You say you are interested in everything. Maybe it's interesting to you. But I'm by no means sure it will be of deep
interest to anybody else. Everyone, of course, will be curious.

Not far from Kuntsevo there's a dark empty house where
my father spent the last twenty years of his life, after the death
of my mother. I have said that the enigma of my father is not
to be deciphered from his possessions, since he gave them no
importance. Could it be that I am wrong? For this house is in

some ways like his life during those last twenty years. But it has no associations for me. I never liked it.

Miron Merzhanov, who built my father several *dachas* in the south, built the house in 1934. It was a wonderful, airy, modern, one-story *dacha* set in a garden, among woods and flowers. The roof was a vast sun deck where I loved to run and play. I remember how the whole family came out to see the new house and how noisy and cheerful it was. My mother's sister, Anna, and her husband, Stanislav (Stakh) Redens, came there. So did my mother's brother, Uncle Pavel (Pavlusha), and his wife Evgenia. Uncle Alexander (Alyosha) and Aunt Maria Svanidze were there, too, and my brothers Yakov (Yasha) and Vasily (Vasya). Things were still going along just as they had before. The house was happy and full of people as it had been in my mother's day. Everybody brought their children. The children shouted and played, and my father enjoyed it very much. My mother's parents came, too. It's not true that after my mother died her family repudiated my father. On the contrary, they all did their best to make him happy. They treated him with consideration, and he was cordial and kind to them all.

But Beria's pince-nez was already gleaming in a corner somewhere, though he was still humble and inconspicuous. He came up from Georgia from time to time to "pay homage" to my father and to look at the new *dacha*. Everyone close to us hated him, starting with the Redenses and the Svanidzes, who knew his work in the Georgian Cheka[1] only too well. Everyone in the family loathed him and felt a premonition of fear, especially my mother, who, as my father himself told me, "made scenes" and insisted as early as 1929 that "that man must not be allowed to set foot in our house."

My father told me about it later, when I was grown up: "I asked her what was wrong with him. Give me facts. I'm not

convinced. I see no facts! But she just cried out, 'What facts do
you need? I just see he's a scoundrel! I won't have him here!'
I told her to go to hell. He's my friend. He's a good Chekist.
He helped us forestall the Mingrelian uprising[2] in Georgia.
I trust him. Facts, facts are what I need!"

My poor, clever mother. The facts came later.

Back in 1934, at the *dacha* in Kuntsevo, we had plenty of
visitors. We were happy then.

One wouldn't know the house now. My father had it rebuilt
over and over again. Probably he was just unable to find peace
of mind, for the same thing happened with all his houses. He
would go south to one of his vacation retreats, and by the time
he went back the next summer the place would have been rebuilt all over again. Either there was too little sunshine for him
or it needed a terrace in the shade. If there was one floor it
needed two, and if there were two, well, better tear one down.

Thus it was with the *dacha* at Kuntsevo. There are two floors
now. No one ever lived on the second, since my father was all
alone. Did he, perhaps, want me and my brother and the grandchildren to live there? I don't know. If so, he never mentioned
it. He built the second floor in 1948. The following year he
held a large reception in the big room there for a delegation
of visitors from China. The second floor was never used again.

My father lived on the ground floor. He lived in one room,
in fact, and made it do for everything. He slept on the sofa,
made up at night as a bed, and had telephones on the table
beside it. The large dining table was piled high with documents, newspapers and books. He used one end for eating
when he was alone. There was a sideboard for china, and it had
medicines in one of the compartments. My father picked out
his medicines himself, since the only doctor he trusted was
Vinogradov, whom he called once or twice a year. The great,
soft rug and the fireplace were all the luxury my father wanted.

The other rooms, which Merzhanov originally designed as a separate office, bedroom and dining room, were all exactly like this one. Once in a while my father moved into one of them and rearranged it in his usual way.

After the war, during my father's last years, the whole Politburo came for dinner nearly every night. They ate in the main room, where my father also saw visitors. I seldom went into this one, and the only foreigner I saw there was Josip Broz Tito in 1946. But all the other leaders of the foreign Communist parties—English, American, French and Italian—have been there, very likely. It was in this room that my father lay in March, 1953. A sofa by the wall was his deathbed.

Once Merzhanov made a "nursery" of several rooms, but later they were converted into a single room as impersonal as all the rest, with its sofa, table and rug. What had been a bedroom became a bare passageway. It had a bookcase and a wardrobe. The piano was there, too, as it annoyed my father in the main room. When and why the piano appeared I have no idea —I don't think it was ever used.

What I liked about the house was the wonderful garden and terraces on every side. My father spent every day from spring to fall out on the terraces. During his later years he was especially fond of the small terrace on the west side where he could watch the setting sun. The terrace faced on a garden. A small, glassed-in veranda that had been built after the war looked out on a garden with flowering cherries.

The garden, the flowers and the woods that surrounded the *dacha* were my father's hobby and relaxation. He never dug in the earth or took a shovel in his hands the way real gardeners do. But he liked things to be cultivated and kept up. He liked the blossoms to be abundant. He liked to see ripe red cherries, apples and tomatoes everywhere, and he expected the gardener to feel the same way. Once in a while he took a pair of shears and pruned a twig or two, but that was the extent of his gardening. Scattered throughout the garden and woods, which were mowed and kept up like a park, were little summerhouses. Some had roofs and others were open to the sky. Some were nothing but a wooden floor with a table, a deck chair, a wicker chaise longue. My father spent hours roaming the garden as if he were seeking a quiet, comfortable spot and not finding it. In summer he spent days at a time wandering out of doors and had his official documents, newspapers and tea brought to him in the park. This was luxury as he wanted and understood it. It showed his healthy appetite for life, his enduring love of nature and the soil. It showed his common sense, too, for in later years he wanted to continue in good health and live longer.

The time I was at Kuntsevo two months before he died, I had a nasty surprise. There were blown-up magazine photographs of children all over the walls, a boy skiing, a girl drinking goat's milk from a horn, children under cherry trees and so on. There was practically a gallery of drawings—reproductions, not even originals—by the artist Yar-Kravchenko in the big room. They were supposed to be likenesses of writers like Gorky and Sholokhov and others I can't remember. There was also a framed reproduction of Repin's[3] famous "Reply of the Zaporozhe Cossacks to the Sultan" in the main room. My father loved this picture and took great pleasure in reciting the obscene reply itself to anyone who happened to be handy. Even higher on the wall there was a portrait of Lenin, by no means one of the best.

It was all weird and surprising to me, since my father had never cared at all about pictures and photographs. The sole exception was the apartment in Moscow. After my mother died, huge photographs of her were hung in my father's office and the dining room there. But my father wasn't living there at the time, and it didn't mean anything. The idea that Stalin lived in the Kremlin is a false one. I can't imagine who thought it up. It is true only in the sense that my father's office and work were in the Kremlin, in the building of the Presidium of the Central Committee and the Council of Ministers.

Strange things happened at Kuntsevo after my father died. The very next day—it was well before the funeral—Beria had the whole household, servants and bodyguards, called together and told that my father's belongings were to be removed right away—no one had any idea where—and that they were all to quit the premises.

Nobody argued with Beria. Men and women who didn't have the slightest idea what was happening and who were practically in a state of shock packed up my father's possessions, his books and furniture and china, and tearfully loaded them onto trucks. They were all carted off somewhere, to the sort of warehouse the secret police had plenty of.[4] Servants who had worked for my father devotedly for ten or fifteen years were simply thrown out. Every one of them was sent away. A good many officers of the bodyguard were transferred to other cities. Two of them shot themselves. No one knew what was going on or what they were guilty of or why they were being picked on. But in the Ministry of State Security, of which, under the system my father had himself unfortunately approved, all his household staff were employees, everyone was required to obey unquestioningly any order from above. I was not consulted about any of this at the time and learned of it only much later.

In 1955, when Beria himself had "fallen," they started restoring the *dacha*. My father's things were brought back. The former servants and commandants were invited back and helped put everything where it belonged and make the house look as it had before. They were preparing to open a museum, like the one in Lenin's house at Leninskiye Gorki.[5] But then came the Twentieth Party Congress.[6] After that, of course, any thought of a museum was dropped. The service buildings in which my father's bodyguards used to live are now a hospital or sanatorium. But the house itself is gloomy, closed up, dead. Sometimes I have a nightmare about this house and the forbidding rooms that always seemed empty, and I wake up cold with fright.

The road there from Poklonnaya Gora is a tree-lined alley now, where residents of the new buildings on Kutuzov Boulevard go for relaxation. From the highway leading to the university you can see how the woods that surround the house have grown dense and wild. This is a house of gloom, a somber monument. Not for anything in the world would I go there now! Is it perhaps, after all, a fitting memorial to what we call the "era of the cult of personality"? My father loved this house. It reflects his taste and he liked it there. Maybe his soul, so restless everywhere else, still longs for shelter under its roof. It would be a natural enough place for it to dwell.

But once upon a time we had another house, too. Imagine that at one time we lived in quite a different house, a house that was sunny and gay, filled with the sounds of children's voices and cheerful, openhearted people. This was the house my mother created and presided over, a house that was filled with her presence. In this house my father was neither a god nor a "cult," but just the father of a family. Named Zubalovo, after the prerevolutionary owner, it is a little over a mile from where I am now, not far from Usovo and less than twenty miles from the center of Moscow.

My parents made it their home from 1919 until my mother died in 1932. Afterward, my father couldn't bear to remain either there or in their old apartment in the city. He took over another apartment in the Kremlin, where we children lived without him. For himself, he built the new *dacha* at Kuntsevo.

As for us, children, grandparents and the rest of the family—
at least until some of them were arrested and sent away—we
spent summers as before at Zubalovo. But without my mother
nothing was the same. Life was changed out of all recognition.

Let me tell you about the life created and supervised by
my mother. Those cloudless years were a fairy tale. I spent them
nearby, not far from this very place. Do you see now why I
can't tear myself away from Zhukovka, where I am sitting in
the woods and writing this?

→»» *3*

The house in which I spent my childhood once belonged to
the younger Zubalov, an oil magnate from Batum. He and
his father were related to Maindorf, the owner of an estate in
Barvikha whose German Gothic house, now a club, still stands
overlooking the lake. The whole area was Maindorf's. So was
the sawmill near Usovo, close by the site of the famous "Gorky
Two" poultry farm. The Usovo railway station, the post office,
the track to the sawmill that now is dilapidated and overgrown,
the whole wonderful forest as far as Odintsovo, once cared for
by a German forester who planted rows of fir where horseback
riders used to go—all of it once belonged to Maindorf. The
Zubalovs owned the two estates near Usovo station, with their
identical gabled houses of German design surrounded by massive brick walls with tile on top.

The Zubalovs also owned oil refineries in Baku and Batum. Theirs was a familiar name to my father and Mikoyan, who led strikes and ran study groups for workers in these same refineries in the beginning of the 1900's. In 1919, after the Revolution, when a chance came to use the many abandoned *dachas* and estates outside Moscow, they both remembered the name Zubalov. Mikoyan and his family, Voroshilov, Shaposhnikov[1] and several other Old Bolshevik families, all lived in Zubalovo Two, as it was called, while my father and mother took over the nearby, and smaller, Zubalovo Four.

The Mikoyans' house to this day is exactly as the exiled owners left it. On the porch is a marble statue of a dog, the former owner's favorite. Inside are marble statues imported from Italy. The walls are hung with Gobelins, and downstairs the windows are of stained glass. The garden, the park, the tennis court, the orangery, stables and greenhouses are all exactly as they have always been. I've always enjoyed going to see our old and good friends in their charming house. I love the dining room with its carved sideboard and old-fashioned chandelier, and the antique clock on the mantelpiece. I like to watch Anastas Mikoyan's ten grandchildren playing on the lawns and afterward picnicking at the very same table under the trees where their parents used to eat. I love going there, where my mother also used to go on visits to Mikoyan's late wife.

Our place, on the other hand, underwent endless transformations. At the outset my father had the woods surrounding the house cleared and half the trees cut down. He had clearings made, and it became lighter, warmer and not so damp. He kept the woods cleared and tended, and had the dead leaves raked up in spring. In front of the house stood a lovely grove of young birches, all shimmering and white, where we children gathered mushrooms every year. Nearby were an

apiary and two open spaces that in summer were sown to buck-
wheat, so the bees could make honey. Strips of open land had
been left beside the tall, dry pine forest. This land, too, was
kept up meticulously. Wild strawberries and blackberries grew
there and the air had a special fragrance.

Only later, when I was older, did I understand the special
quality of my father's interest in nature and see that it was a
practical and at bottom a profoundly peasant interest. He was
unable merely to contemplate nature; he had to work it and be
forever transforming it. He had fruit trees planted over large
tracts and strawberry, raspberry and currant bushes planted in
abundance. A small open space at a distance from the house
was enclosed by chicken wire and neatly hedged with shrubs
to make a run for turkeys, pheasant and guinea fowl. Ducks
paddled in a little pond. All this did not spring up overnight
but developed bit by bit, so that we children grew up on what
was actually a small estate with a country routine of its own—
haying, picking mushrooms and berries, our own fresh honey
every year, our own pickles and preserves, our own poultry.

My father was actually more interested in these things than
my mother. She only wanted to make sure that the enormous
lilac bushes outside the house bloomed properly every spring.
She planted a row of mock oranges under the balcony and saw
that I had a little garden of my own where my nurse showed
me how to dig and plant nasturtiums and marigolds.

My mother was interested in something else—our education
and upbringing. Although I was only six and a half when she
died, I could already read and write both Russian and German.
I could draw and model in clay and make cutouts with scissors
and glue. I could read music and write down the notes as a
tune was played on the piano. My brother and I were lucky,
for our mother found remarkable teachers for us. (I'll tell you
about my nurse later.) This was especially important in the

case of my brother Vasily, who was already a difficult child. Vasily had a wonderful tutor, Alexander Muravyov, who was forever thinking up fascinating expeditions to the river and woods: fishing, camping out all night by the river in a lean-to and cooking fish, nut-picking and mushroom-gathering expeditions and all kinds of others besides. Of course, all these things had a purpose and were combined with reading, drawing and other lessons, with raising rabbits and hedgehogs and garter snakes and other useful activities.

Winter and summer a teacher named Natalia Konstantinovna—no one called them governesses any more—took turns with Alexander Muravyov and spent alternate days teaching us clay modeling, showing us how to make our own toys out of wood, how to color and draw and do other things. She also taught us German, and her lessons, entertaining and full of play, were unforgettable. She was a teacher of real talent.

All this educational machinery whirred and spun and was set in motion by my mother, yet she herself was practically never home. It was not the thing at that time for a woman, especially a woman Party member, to spend much time with her children. My mother worked first on the staff of a magazine and then enrolled in the Industrial Academy. She was forever attending meetings somewhere, and she spent all her free time with my father. He was her whole life. We children generally had to be content with her simply checking on our progress. She was strict and she had high standards. I cannot recall her kissing or caressing me ever. She was afraid of spoiling me because my father petted and spoiled me enough as it was. Of course, we had no idea that we owed all our games and amusements, our whole happy childhood, to her. We only realized it later, when she was no longer there.

What splendid children's parties we had! All the Kremlin children would be asked, twenty or thirty of them. There were a lot of people living in the Kremlin then, and all of them were on easy, straightforward terms. We always gave our own little play or entertainment, which we spent weeks rehearsing ahead of time under the supervision of Alexander Muravyov and Natalia Konstantinovna.

I remember my last birthday party while my mother was still alive. It was February, 1932, and I was six years old. The Kremlin apartment was filled with children. We recited verses in Russian and German and satirical couplets about shock workers and political double-dealers. We danced the Ukrainian gopak in folk costumes we'd made ourselves out of colored paper and stiff cotton netting. Artyom Sergeyev, a friend of my brother Vasily's and now a much-decorated general, crouched on all fours in a bearskin and growled while somebody read a fable by Krylov.[2] The audience screamed with delight. The walls were festooned with the drawings and wall newspapers we had made. Later the whole crowd, parents and children alike, went to the dining room for tea and cake and candies. My father was there, too. He was only watching, of course, but it amused him. Once in a while he enjoyed the sounds of children playing.

It's all etched into my memory forever. What a playground we had in the woods at Zubalovo! We had a seesaw and swings and a wooden tree house, suspended between three pines, which you could only reach by a rope ladder! We always had other children staying with us. Either Artyom Sergeyev or Tolya Ronin* shared Vasily's room with him practically all the time, while I often had Olya Stroyev,† the daughter of one of my mother's old friends, staying with me. Svetlana Bukharin, "Kozya," as she was called, and her mother, Esfir Gurvich, generally spent the summer with us.

---

* An officer who died in the war.
† A well-known Soviet geneticist.

The house was always full. Nikolai Bukharin,[3] whom everyone adored, often came for the summer. He filled the whole
house with animals, which he loved. Hedgehogs would be
chasing each other across the balcony, garter snakes sunning
themselves in jars, a tame fox racing through the park and a
crippled hawk glaring from a cage. I vaguely remember Bukharin in a long blouse and linen trousers and sandals. He used
to play with the children and tease my nurse, whom he taught
to ride a bicycle and shoot an air rifle. Everyone had a good
time when he was around. Years later, long after he was dead,
"Bukharin's fox" was still racing around the Kremlin, which
was empty and desolate by that time, and hiding from the
people in the Tainitsky Garden.

Sergo Ordzhonikidze[4] and his wife Zina—he was very close
to my father, and she to my mother—stayed with us for long
stretches at Zubalovo. I won't even try to name all the people
who came and visited us there. Many I don't remember because I was so small. And I do not want to ask other people,
who do remember. I want to put down only what I know and
remember and saw myself.

The grownups often had parties of their own on birthdays
and holidays. The colorful Semyon Budyonny[5] would bring
his accordion and play Russian and Ukrainian songs. Budyonny and Voroshilov had especially good voices. My father
would sing, too. He had a fine ear and a clear, high-pitched
voice. (His speaking voice, on the other hand, was a monotone,
low and not very loud.) I have no idea whether or not my
mother could sing, but it is said that once in a long, long while
she would dance a graceful Georgian *lezghinka*. Otherwise,
however, we paid no special attention to anything Georgian
—my father had become completely Russian.

In those days people didn't care much about the so-called
national question, being concerned mainly with the qualities

that people of all cultures have in common. My brother Vasily, for example, said to me one time, "You know, Papa used to be a Georgian once." Being only six, I had no idea what this meant, so he explained: "They went around in long Circassian cloaks and cut everybody up with daggers." That was all we knew at the time about our Georgian origins. My father was always furious when friends appeared from Georgia bearing, as Georgians will, gifts in the form of fruit and wine. Since my father had banned them, they would all be sent back and my mother, "that Russian woman," would get the blame. My mother was actually born and grew up in the Caucasus. She loved Georgia and knew it well. But she, too, gave no encouragement to this "generosity" at the public expense.

Our apartment in the Kremlin was run by a housekeeper, a German from Riga, Latvia, named Carolina Till, who was one of my mother's finds. She was a charming old woman, neat and immaculate and very kind, who wore her hair piled high on her head in the old-fashioned way, in combs and with a chignon on the crown. My mother entrusted the whole of our rather modest budget to her, and with it she ran the household and saw to meals. I am referring, of course, to the period I actually remember, about 1929 to 1933. By this time my mother had finally established a routine and the at least elementary comfort which was all the budget of even the highest Party leaders would allow. She ran the household herself on ration cards, and neither we nor anybody else had servants. Up to 1933, then, our household was run in a perfectly normal way, by my mother or by a housekeeper, without any sign of Chekists or bodyguards. The only guard was a man who rode in the car with my father and had nothing to do with the house. He wasn't allowed anywhere near it.

All the Soviet leaders lived pretty much like this at that time. No one cared about luxury or possessions, though they did try to give a good education to their children. They hired good governesses of the old, prerevolutionary school, mainly to teach their children German. All the wives had jobs and read all they could in their spare time. Sports had just come into style. All of them played tennis, and they had tennis courts and croquet lawns at their *dachas*. The women paid no attention to makeup or clothes, but they looked nice just the same.

In summer my parents went to Sochi[6]—this had become a regular thing with them. The first time they took me was in 1930 or 1931. We stayed in a small *dacha* near Matsesta, where my father was taking warm baths for his rheumatism. It was only after my mother died that they started building him special *dachas*. My mother didn't live to see all this luxury, paid for out of limitless public funds. That happened after she died, when the house came to be run at state expense, on a military footing, by agents of the secret police. During my mother's lifetime we had a normal, modest life.

During those far-off years my parents always went south with friends, with Abel Yenukidze,[7] my mother's godfather and a great friend of them both, with Mikoyan, Voroshilov or Molotov[8] and all their wives and children. I still have pictures of happy summer picnics on which they'd all go together by car and everything was cheerful and simple. Sometimes my father went hawk shooting with a double-barreled rifle. Or he might go hunting hares at night from an automobile. Bowling, billiards, *gorodki*[9]—anything that took a sharp eye, he was good at. He never swam; he didn't know how. He didn't like sitting in the sun either. The one thing he did like was to go walking in the shade of the woods. But even this quickly bored him, and he preferred stretching out in a deck chair with a book and his documents or the newspapers. And he could sit at the table with guests by the hour. It was the custom of the Caucasus in him to sit for hours at a time, not so much eating or drinking as simply sitting over the dishes discussing and arguing and reaching decisions.

My mother was used to this and had no interest in the usual relaxations of her age and sex. In this sense she was a perfect wife. In Moscow once while I was a baby and she was still nursing me, my father fell slightly ill at Sochi. Even on this occasion she left me without the least hesitation to my nurse and my goat Nyuska and went off to my father. Her place was there rather than with her child.

In short, we had a home just like other people, with friends, relatives, children and family holidays. It was true of our apartment in the city, and it was especially true of Zubalovo in summer. My father transformed Zubalovo from a dark country place that was densely overgrown, with a gloomy gabled house and a lot of old furniture, into a sunny, abundant estate with flower and vegetable gardens and all sorts of useful outbuildings. The house was rebuilt and the high Gothic gables removed; the rooms were remodeled and the musty old furniture carted away. The only things that remained were some chairs and a table and a tall mirror in a gilt frame with carved gilt feet in my mother's little room upstairs.

My mother and father lived upstairs, and the children and my grandmother, grandfather and anyone who happened to be staying with us, downstairs. In summer our life was centered on the terrace downstairs and on my father's balcony on the second floor. My nurse was forever sending me there. "Go take these currants to Papa" or "Bring Papa some violets" or "Take him some lilies of the valley." I would go trotting off and be rewarded no matter what I brought by a warm, tobacco-scented kiss from my father and a word of mild admonition from my mother.

In spite of her youth my mother, who was thirty years old in 1931, was respected by the entire household. She was very much loved by everyone. She was intelligent, beautiful, extraordinarily gentle and considerate in every relationship. At the same time she could be firm, stubborn and unyielding when she felt that a conviction could not be compromised. No one but she could have brought about unity, even harmony, in a family of such strikingly varied personalities. She was the acknowledged head of the household.

My mother was very tender and loving with my oldest brother Yakov, my father's son by his first wife, Yekaterina Svanidze. Yakov, who was only seven years younger than she, loved and respected her greatly in return. She did all she could to ease his hard life. She helped him in his first marriage and stood up for him against our father, who had always treated Yakov unfairly and with a coldness he did not deserve. My mother was on the friendliest terms with all the Svanidzes, with Sashiko (Alexandra) and Mariko (Maria), the sisters of my father's first wife, who had died young, with her brother, Alexander Svanidze, and his wife Maria. My mother's parents and her brothers, my Uncles Fyodor (Fedya) and Pavel, her sister Anna and Anna's husband, Stanislav Redens, all were at our house constantly like one big, friendly family. There were no quarrels, no petty squabbles, no narrow-mindedness or meanness of any kind. My father was surrounded on all sides by relatives who had seen life for what it is and had worked in the most varied fields. Each of them brought to the house his own ideas and experiences. My father could not have been cut off from life in those years. That came later, when he was isolated from all the sincere, honest, kindly members of the family who had been on an equal footing with him.

Alexander Svanidze was a major figure in Soviet finance who lived and worked a great deal abroad, in London, Geneva, Berlin. He was one of the old Marxists, who were highly educated and at home in the culture of Europe. Uncle Pavel was a soldier

who had had considerable experience in the Civil War, on the
General Staff and in the Military Academy. Redens was a colleague of Dzerzhinsky's[10] and an old and experienced Chekist.
Their wives, too, Aunt Maria, an opera singer, my sharp-
tongued Aunt Evgenia, my Aunt Anna and even my grandparents, Old Bolsheviks that they were, all brought my father
news, and sometimes he even asked them for a "bit of gossip."
All of them were incorruptible and had no special axes to
grind. They formed a circle that sprang up around my mother
and vanished soon after she died, not so quickly at first, but
finally and irrevocably by 1937.

Each of them ought to be described separately. They were
extraordinary personalities, gifted and fascinating. The life
of almost every one was cut short in some tragic fashion. Not
one of them had a chance to live his talented and interesting
life to the end. If only out of respect for their memory, from
love and profound gratitude for what they were to me in that
place of sunshine I call my childhood, I ought to tell you about
them. You would have liked all of them if you had seen and
known them.

Moreover, in our time the destinies of the most dissimilar
people are intertwined and woven into a single knot. People's
lives assume astonishing, unexpected shapes; their fortunes
rise and fall. Suddenly, after soaring to the most improbable
heights, they come plummeting down. Neither politics nor
revolution shows any mercy to the lives and fortunes of men.
That is why I believe that family chronicles are worthwhile
after all. They always contain the stuff of which history is
made. Besides, what story in fiction has as much originality
as the story of a real person?

→>> *4*

You will understand my mother and her short life only when
you know about her parents. They, too, had interesting lives,
that were in many ways typical of the time. My mother's ancestry and the whole environment in which her childhood
was spent determined most of her personality.

Grandfather Sergei Alliluyev's memoirs appeared in 1946,
but they were heavily edited and cut. (The original manuscript
is still in the hands of the Marx-Engels-Lenin Institute, pub-
lisher of his book.) Parts of the book were reissued in 1954, in
a version that was even more heavily edited than before. This
edition is wholly lacking in interest.

Grandfather was from a peasant family in the Voronezh
region. His grandmother was a Gypsy—he was not of pure
Russian stock. It must have been from their Gypsy blood

that the Alliluyevs got their southern, somewhat exotic features, their black eyes and flashing white teeth, their dark skins and slender frames. These traits were particularly marked in my mother and her brother Pavel, a real Hindu to look at, resembling the young Nehru. It was probably from the Gypsies, too, that my grandfather derived an unquenchable thirst to be free and a passion for wandering from place to place. He took up metalwork at an early age. He was gifted with his hands and good at all kinds of mechanical work. He became a mechanic and went to work in a railway workshop in Transcaucasia. He formed a lifelong attachment to Georgia, its natural beauty and its southern abundance. He loved the generous profusion of nature in the south, and he had a special feeling for the Georgian, Armenian and Azerbaidzhanian character. He lived in Tiflis,[1] Baku and Batum. In workers' study circles there he met such Social Democrats as Mikhail Kalinin[2] and Ivan Fioletov.[3] In 1898 he joined the Russian Social Democratic Workers' Party.

His memoirs contain a most interesting description of Georgia in those days, including an account of the influence of the radical Russian intelligentsia on the national liberation movement of Georgia and the surprising absence of ethnic rivalry in the revolutionary movement in Transcaucasia, a spirit that later, unfortunately, disappeared. My grandfather was never a theoretician or an important figure in the Party. He was one of the humble rank and file, without whom there could have been no communication between one Party group and another, nor the revolutionary groundwork laid, nor the Revolution itself accomplished.

Later, from the early 1900's, he lived in St. Petersburg with his family and was a skilled worker at the Electric Light Company. He was always a dedicated worker. He was respected as a first-rate mechanic who knew his job to perfection. My grandfather and his family had a four-room apartment in St.

Petersburg. It wasn't large, but it would be as much as a Soviet professor could dream of today. His children went to a high school in St. Petersburg and grew up as members of the real Russian intelligentsia. That's what they were when the Revolution came in 1917. I'll tell you more about them later.

My grandfather continued working in the field of electric power after the Revolution. He built the Shatura Power Station[4] and lived and worked there a long time. At one time he was even Chairman of the Leningrad Electric Power Company. As an Old Bolshevik he was close to the old guard of the Revolution. He was astonishingly sensitive, a gentle, courteous man who got along with everyone, yet was at the same time inwardly strong, proud and incorruptible. To the end of his days—he died in 1945 at the age of seventy-nine—he retained his own strong individuality, his spirit as a revolutionary and idealist of former times, his integrity and his extraordinary honesty and uprightness. Gentle as he was, he could be unyielding with those who didn't accept his high standards.

Tall and in later years thin, with long, lean arms and legs, neat and even a bit distinguished-looking in the Petersburg manner, with a pointed beard and gray mustache, Grandfather looked a little like Kalinin. Small boys on the street sometimes hailed him as "Grandpapa Kalinin!" Even when he was old, his black eyes still had a lively glint in them and he was still capable of bursting into gay, infectious laughter.

Grandfather lived with us at Zubalovo and was adored by all his many grandchildren. He had a carpenter's bench and tools of all kinds in his room, to say nothing of miraculous bits of iron and wire and odds and ends of every sort of which we children were in awe. He let us rummage in his collection and take anything we wanted. Grandfather was always making and soldering things, sharpening and planing and making household repairs, even fixing the electric wiring. Everyone came to him for help and advice in matters of this kind. He loved going on long walks with us children. Uncle Pavel's children, who were living at Zubalovo Two, would come along, or the son of my Aunt Anna, for Grandfather loved to give us all a good time. We would all go to the woods together to gather mushrooms and nuts. I remember Grandfather's taking me on his shoulders when I was tired. And I remember floating above the path, high over all the others, and reaching out with my hands and plucking nuts from the branches.

My mother's death broke my grandfather's spirit. He changed and grew silent and withdrawn. He had always been modest and retiring and had always hated attention. This diffidence, this sensitivity and gentleness were natural qualities of his. But it may be that he had also learned them from the magnificent Russian intelligentsia to whom he was bound by the cause of revolution all his life.

But after 1932 he drew into himself completely. He stayed in his room for days at a time, making things and turning bits of wood on a lathe. And he became gentler than ever with his grandchildren. He divided his time between us and his daughter Anna, but mostly he stayed with us at Zubalovo. Then he fell ill. I suspect it was his spirit that began to ail first and then his body, because he had always had an iron constitution. In 1938 he suffered a new blow, the death of his son Pavel. Meantime in 1937 his son-in-law, Stanislav Redens, had been arrested. After the war, in 1948, his daughter Anna was also sent to prison. Thank God Grandfather didn't live to see it; he died in 1945 of a stomach cancer that was discovered too late. But the fact is that his illnesses were not the illnesses of old age and the flesh but the inward illnesses of the spirit. Yet with that sensitivity and refinement of his, he never burdened anyone with his sufferings or with appeals or requests of any kind.

He began writing his memoirs before the war. He had always loved writing. Even when I was a little girl he used to send me long letters from the Caucasus with detailed descriptions of the southern beauty he loved so much. He had a flowery style, like Gorky, whom he admired very much as a writer, and he agreed with Gorky that every man ought to tell the story of his life. He wrote a great deal and with enthusiasm. Unfortunately he didn't live to see his book published, though his old friend Kalinin strongly recommended it to the publishing house as the work of "one of the oldest of Old Bolsheviks and a born rebel."

His illness went terribly fast the last year, and he grew dreadfully thin. I went to see him in the hospital not long before he died and was shocked. He was no longer able to speak. He just closed his eyes with his hand and silently wept, for he realized that people were coming to say good-bye. He lay in his coffin, later on, like a Hindu holy man, with his thin, withered, beautiful face, his slender, aquiline nose, his beard and mustache of purest white. Many Old Bolsheviks came to the open coffin in the Museum of the Revolution to say good-bye. And at the cemetery, the old revolutionary Litvin-Sedoi[5] made a speech which I didn't fully understand then but have remembered ever since and now understand very well. It began: "We, the older generation of idealistic Marxists . . ."

My grandparents' marriage was a highly romantic one. My grandmother wasn't even fourteen when she tied all her clothes in a bundle, tossed them out the window, slipped out the window herself and ran off with my grandfather, a young worker in Tiflis. But in Georgia, where she was born and grew up, youth and love come early and there was nothing unusual in the story.

What was unusual was the fact that she left a relatively

comfortable home, parents she loved, and a large family of brothers and sisters for an impoverished twenty-year-old mechanic. All her life she kept a photograph of the whole family posed outside the house in a horse-drawn cab—her parents, the house, her favorite horse, a dog stretched out on the ground, the coachman holding the horse by the bridle, and the entire family sitting stiffly in the cab and staring straight at the camera.

Our grandmother, Olga Fedorenko, was born and grew up in Georgia. All her life she loved the country and people as her own. She herself was a strange mixture. Although her father, Evgeny Fedorenko, had a Ukrainian name, his mother was Georgian and he grew up in Georgia and spoke Georgian. But he married Magdalena Eichholz, who was from a family of German settlers. Ever since the reign of Catherine II there had been colonies of Germans in Georgia living in settlements of their own. Magdalena Eichholz was a tavernkeeper. She was the perfect German housewife: she baked fine cakes and bore nine children, of whom our grandmother, Olga, was the youngest. She brought up all nine in the Protestant church. The Fedorenkos spoke German and Georgian. Grandmother only learned Russian later and always spoke it with a Georgian accent, adding various *"vai-mes"* and *"shvilos"* and *"genatsvale-chirimes,"* not to mention *"Jesus Maria"* and, of course, *"Mein Gott!"*

She was always religious, and the revolutionary life she and Grandfather led only cleansed her religious faith of any narrowness or dogmatism. She could see no difference between the Protestant, Gregorian or Armenian, and Orthodox churches and considered such distinctions a waste of time. Whenever we children started making fun of her and asking "Where is God?" or "If man has a soul, where is it?" she'd get angry and tell us, "Wait till you grow up and you'll see where.

Now stop it! You're not going to change my mind." And she
was right. By the time I was thirty-five I realized that Grandmother was wiser than any of us.

Brought up by a hard-working German mother, my grandmother was herself a woman of exceptional industry. She and
Grandfather both had golden hands, but hers were a woman's
skills. She was a wonderful cook and dressmaker and a splendid
manager of the meager resources available to her as the wife
of a Bolshevik who was in jail part of the time and always on
the move from one town to another. Later on you couldn't
fail to see how much she hated seeing our household run like
public property by state employees who were just pouring
government money down the drain! The functionaries who
were running the house didn't understand, or, rather, they
understood only too well and couldn't forgive her for it. Unlike my tactful grandfather, who always held his tongue, she
was quite capable of bursting into sudden screams of abuse
at what she called our "sloppy managers"—all the state-
employed cooks and servants and commandants who looked
on her as a "fussy old freak." We children used to hear this
kind of talk about her, too, when we were all living at Zubalovo
after my mother's death. It wasn't until later, of course, that
we realized that Grandmother had just too hot a temper to
stand silently by while the household was outrageously mis-
managed.

It was not for nothing that Grandmother grew up in Georgia
and loved it there. Her whole approach to life was hot-blooded
and southern. There were endless tears of sorrow and jubila-
tion, there were lamentations and lengthy declarations of love
and tenderness and disapproval. My mother, who was more
restrained, like Grandfather, got tired of Grandmother's out-
pourings and her constant criticisms of the way the household
was run and the children brought up and of my mother herself.

She didn't like Grandmother's living with us so much of the
time and interfering in the household. Could it also be that
Grandmother's heartaches and fears were only too justified,
and that my mother was actually afraid and trying to close her
eyes to it all?

But let me go back. In spite of everything, my grandparents
were a good couple in certain ways. She had had four years of
schooling—the same, very likely, as he. They lived in Tiflis,
Batum and Baku, and in those days my grandmother was a
splendid, forbearing, faithful wife. She was dedicated to the
same causes as he, and she too joined the Party even before the
Revolution. Later she used to complain that "Sergei ruined"
her life and caused her "nothing but suffering."

All four of their children, Anna, Fyodor, Pavel, and
Nadezhda (Nadya), were born in the Caucasus and were
Southerners—in looks, memories and everything a child un-
consciously picks up in the family during his earliest years.
All the children were exceptionally good-looking—all but
Fyodor, who made up for it by being the most intelligent. He
was so gifted that he was admitted to the School for Marine
Honor Guards in St. Petersburg in spite of his lowly origins.
All of them were outgoing, warmhearted and kind. However,
the strongest, staunchest and most implacable was my mother,
who had a special inner steadfastness and fortitude. The
others were much softer. Pavel and Anna were goodness itself,
so that my mother was always complaining that they and our
grandparents "just let the children run wild." They in turn
took her to task for being "too strict" and addicted to governesses, who, they said, "tormented" children and refused to let
them "grow free." But these were just love quarrels. All
four of the Alliluyev children were very close and very fond
of one another.

Grandfather and Grandmother wanted all their children

to have as much education as possible, so once they were settled in St. Petersburg the children were sent to high school. One is struck in the photographs of those years by how good-looking my grandmother was. It wasn't simply the oval face with its large gray eyes, regular features and small, refined mouth, but her surprisingly fine carriage, straight, open, proud, what is called "regal," altogether a bearing of extraordinary dignity. Somehow it made her large eyes seem larger and her small figure taller. She was very short, with fair skin and light hair, well built, neat and quick-moving. It is said that she was unusually attractive, so that there was no coping with all her admirers.

To tell the truth, she was easily infatuated. From time to time she hurled herself into an affair—with a Pole, a Hungarian, a Bulgarian, even a Turk; she liked southern men very much and sometimes complained angrily that "Russian men are boors." Her children were students in high school by that time. They took it all with patience and good humor. Each time it would end and the family settle back into its normal routine.

In later years my grandmother and grandfather suffered so much from my mother's death, each in his own way, that they lived apart, in separate apartments. In summer, meeting at dinner in our house at Zubalovo, they would start quarreling over nothing. Grandfather would be particularly irritated at her finding fault with household details. He'd outgrown it all, somehow. He was busy with his memoirs, and these annoying complaints, these ohs and ahs and Caucasus-type laments over little things, upset him.

Both of them, as a result, met old age, illness and death alone and in their own ways. Both remained true to themselves, their own characters and interests. Both had their own outlooks and pride. They refused to cling to one another as helpless old people do. Each loved to be free. And although both of them suffered and were lonely, neither wanted to give up any freedom in the final years of his life. "Freedom, freedom, I love freedom!" Grandmother loved to exclaim. What she meant, secretly but quite obviously, too, was that it was Grandfather who had robbed her of her freedom and "ruined" her life.

Besides running a household, bringing up four children and making all their clothes, my grandmother also took a course and became an excellent midwife. She loved life and she loved children. She thought midwifery was wonderful work. It gave her tremendous satisfaction.

After the First World War broke out, she went to work in a hospital caring for wounded soldiers. All her life she treasured her letters from soldiers who had gotten well and gone home. She showed them to me with love and emotion. All through the war she worked at home, too, making underwear for soldiers. She did it, as she did everything, with the skill of a professional.

For all their "golden hands" and their industriousness, both my grandparents were utterly impractical. During later years when they took turns living first with Anna Serveyevna and then with us, at Zubalovo, and had some small token privileges, such as ration books, to which Old Bolsheviks were entitled, both of them continued to show the utmost scorn for worldly goods. They kept on wearing the same old clothing left over from before the Revolution. They would wear the same overcoat for twenty years, and out of three old dresses my grandmother would make a perfectly good new one. It wasn't that they were hypocrites or ascetics, but merely that they had no interest in material things and were wholly unaware of their high position in our new society. The relatives of other important men in the Party, meantime, were using similar positions to carve out lives of luxury for themselves and their relations, both close and not so close.

Such a thing never even occurred to my grandparents. My

mother, too, was exceedingly modest in her requirements. Toward the end of her life, but only then, she was given a few good dresses by Pavel, who was working in the Soviet mission in Berlin. She looked wonderful in them. But most of the time she went around in the simplest homemade things and only once in a great while ordered a "best" dress from a dressmaker.

This lack of the acquisitive spirit and even innocence that such a thing existed was annoying to some people. "Look at that wretched old pair," they'd say. "Can't their son-in-law get them something better to wear?" Their son-in-law, meanwhile, wore a plain military tunic of linen in summer and of wool in winter and an overcoat that was fifteen years old. He also had a short, strange-looking fur coat with squirrel on the inside and reindeer on the outside, which he started wearing soon after the Revolution. He went on wearing it with a fur cap to the very end of his days.

My father had known the Alliluyevs a long time, since the end of the 1890's. He loved and respected them both, and they felt the same way toward him. In his reminiscences my grandfather has dealt at length with their early meetings, which had to do with the underground workers' circles, and I won't repeat what he has written.

There is a family legend that as a young man my father rescued my mother from drowning. It happened in Baku when she was two years old. She was playing on the shore and fell in. He is said to have gone in after her and fished her out. Years afterward my mother met my father again. She was a schoolgirl of sixteen by that time, and he an old friend of the family, a thirty-eight-year-old revolutionary just back from exile in Siberia. Maybe the fact that he had rescued her seemed significant to her, for she was a romantic, full of feeling and imagination.

What do I remember? Only that my grandparents stayed

with us constantly at Zubalovo, though their rooms were at
opposite ends of the house. That they had dinner with my
father, and that Grandfather would speak to him in the familiar way, as "thee" or "thou," while Grandmother used
the less familiar "you." And that my father was exceedingly
deferential and addressed them both by their first names
and their patronymics. It was the same way after my mother
died. My grandparents took her death terribly hard. They
understood only too well how much my father must be suffering. And so, it seemed to me then and still seems to me now,
looking back, nothing in their attitude changed. No one spoke
openly of the pain all three of them shared, but it was always
imperceptibly present. Maybe that's why later, when the
household broke up and meetings among the former members
became less frequent, my father seemed more and more to be
avoiding my grandparents. He kept seeing them until the
war, on his rare visits to Zubalovo. It was generally in summer.
They would all gather at a picnic table in the woods, out in
the open air, and have a meal. But my father must have found
these visits too poignant a reminder of the past—he was
usually cross and unhappy by the time he left. Sometimes he'd
quarrel with someone or lose his temper at one of the children
for no good reason at all.

Grandfather used to come to our apartment in the Kremlin
and sit in my room by the hour waiting for my father. Dinner
was at seven or eight at night, whenever my father appeared
after a day in his office at the Central Committee or the Council of Ministers, the Council of People's Commissars as it was
called then. He was never alone. At best, Grandfather might
get to sit at the table with him, in silence. Sometimes my
father teased him about his memoirs. But on the whole he
respected the old man and refrained from crude jokes about
them. At times, when my father had brought too many people,

Grandfather would sigh and say, "I guess I'll go home. I'll come another time." But he found it so painful that it might be six months or a year before he came again.

So strong were Grandfather's scruples that he never once asked my father what had happened to his son-in-law Redens, though the fate of his daughter Anna, her shattered life and the lives of her sons worried him deeply. He simply suffered in silence and whistled to himself a little, as was his way. He had too much pride ever to ask for anything, or plead or beg. People without dignity or pride had no idea what to make of it. What! To be with someone like my father and never ask for a thing? The fact is, he never did.

In this respect Grandmother was simpler and more natural. She always had a pile of complaints and requests that had to do with practical matters. In the old days she used to go to Lenin, who knew and respected the whole family, and later she turned to my father. And although War Communism[6] and the worst of the devastation were long past, Grandmother was often in need of the barest essentials because she was unable to adjust to the new way of life. My mother had all sorts of scruples about appealing to my father on her parents' behalf. And so Grandmother, who was altogether unable to cope, frequently turned directly to my father with her requests. "Ah, Josef, imagine, I can't get vinegar anywhere!" My father would burst out laughing and my mother would fume. My father would have the whole thing settled in a second.

Once my mother died Grandmother no longer felt at home in our house. She lived either at Zubalovo or in an immaculate little apartment of her own in the Kremlin, alone with a lot of old photographs and possessions that she had carried with her from one town to another all her life. There were the threadbare old Caucasus rugs, the ubiquitous wide sofa from the Caucasus that was covered with a rug and cushions and had a rug hanging on the wall above it. There were ancient chests and some cheap trinkets from St. Petersburg. Everything was neat, clean, in perfect order. I liked going there, for it was quiet and cozy and warm. But it was also infinitely sad. What did she have to talk of but sorrows?

She had boundless health and vitality. She was wonderful-looking even at seventy. Tiny as she was, she always held her head high and proud, and this made her seem taller. She always had on a fresh, neat dress that she had made herself out of something old. Her hair was always perfect, and she always wore amber beads around her left wrist. In a word, she was as beautiful as ever. She had no wrinkles and no signs of age. In her later years she started suffering from a weak heart, partly as a result of afflictions of the spirit. She never could understand why her daughter Anna should be in prison, and she was tormented by it. She'd give me letters for my father and later take them back. She knew it wouldn't do any good. She was fatalistic about the catastrophes that had befallen the family one after the other, as though it couldn't have been any other way.

In the early spring of 1951 she died unexpectedly of a heart attack at the age of seventy-six.

Even when they were old and lonely, she and Grandfather never burdened people with their troubles. They were gracious and discreet with outsiders, and as a result hardly anyone was aware of what they were going through. The Spanish have a saying for old men and women like them: "The trees die standing."

Now that my son is grown and I'll be a grandmother in two or three years, I'm sorry I didn't understand sooner. Do grandsons and granddaughters ever understand grandparents, or children their parents? We thought Grandmother was a cantankerous old woman; we loved Grandfather better. Yet in their different ways they were both apostles of innocence and truth. Can we, their grandsons and granddaughters, claim to be any better?

→>> *5*

Yes, those old trees died standing. Each of their children came to a tragic end. Life broke them all in different ways. Was it the fate of everyone at that time? Or were they merely too weak to bear the weight of history, which has, after all, broken far more powerful trunks and ripped up centuries-old trees by the roots? At least none of them ran from his age and time. On the contrary, they were all in the thick of things. The private life of each of them was swallowed up by the events that were going on around them.

My mother's favorite brother, Pavel, who was closer to her and more like her than anyone in the family, only gentler and more easygoing, became a professional soldier.

I say "became" because he didn't choose to be one. The

Revolution and the Civil War started and he went off to fight. He saw action everywhere, at Archangel, in Turkestan, against the counterrevolutionaries in Central Asia called the Basmachi, against the English and the White Guards. When the Civil War was over Lenin ordered him on Urvantsev's[1] Far Northern expedition to prospect for coal and iron ore. His functions were strictly auxiliary—he was a soldier and not a scientist after all. But someone had to protect the scientists in that wild and remote region. The expedition discovered gigantic coal and iron ore deposits on the Norilka River just as Urvantsev had predicted. The city of Norilsk is there now. There are multistory houses, movie theaters, an outdoor swimming pool and enormous stores. But in those days the members of the expedition lived in tents and rode reindeer, and it was very much like a Jack London novel. Pavel's children still have pictures of the reindeer, the dogs, the clothing that was of fur both inside and out, the vast expanse of white desert. Urvantsev is still alive and in Leningrad. Perhaps he has written or is planning to write about his great achievement.

Uncle Pavel was sent at the end of the twenties as our military representative to what was then pre-Nazi Germany. Officially he was attached to our trade mission. He and his family lived there until 1933.

My mother must have missed him very much—it was the hardest time in her life. Sometimes he sent her a dress or some good perfume, the kind of thing every woman likes, though people led austere lives in those days and didn't give much thought to the amenities. But my father took a puritanical view of what he called "foreign luxury" and refused to tolerate even the scent of perfume. In his opinion the only fragrance that was becoming to a woman was her own freshness and cleanliness. And so my mother had to enjoy these presents surreptitiously, although she did wear the perfume. In fact, I don't remember her ever being without it. She always gave off a marvelous fragrance. Sometimes she came to my room to stroke my head as I was falling asleep and to say good night. As I lay there I could smell the exotic perfume on my pillow for hours afterward.

One time my mother went to Karlovy Vary, then known as Karlsbad, and also spent a short time with her brother in Berlin. Some wonderful things appeared in the house for me and Vasily after that—sweaters and underwear and all sorts of things that were an unheard-of luxury for those years. To keep us from "falling under the baneful influence of bourgeois Europe," we were told that our mother had brought them from Leningrad. For a long time we believed it. To the end of his days my father would ask me with a look of real displeasure, "Is that something foreign you've got there?" He beamed whenever I told him, no, it had been made in the Soviet Union. This went on long after I was grown. And if, heaven forbid, I happened to be wearing perfume, he'd frown with disgust and mumble, "What are you doing wearing that stuff!"

There was no need to make a Puritan of my mother—her tastes were simple enough already. Besides, in those days it was a matter of course for the leaders, especially leaders of the Party, to live in what was almost puritanical style. Out of the kindness of his heart, her brother just wanted to spoil her a little now and then.

Unfortunately Uncle Pavel was in Germany when my mother died. There was nothing he could do but find strength to accept the terrible blow.

Later he lived in Moscow. I always remember him in uniform. He was the equivalent of a general in the Tank Section of the People's Commissariat of Defense,[2] which he helped found. He was slender, tall and long-legged, like Grandfather, with brown eyes that were melancholy and astonishingly gentle and kind. He adored Vasily and me, especially after our mother died, and was forever taking one or the other of us on his lap and kissing us and whispering to us affectionately.

Later, not long before his death in 1938, he used to come to our apartment in the Kremlin and sit by the hour in Vasily's room or mine and wait for my father the way Grandfather and my Uncle Alexander Svanidze did. He must have found it difficult and upsetting, for he would sigh and was obviously in low spirits. I remember, too, how he'd come to my father's *dacha* at Blizhny with his wife and children and the rest of our relatives for New Year's and family birthdays. My father was very fond of Pavel and the children. Dinner would be as jolly as in any other family where the members are very close.

In 1938, after Alexander Svanidze and his wife and my Aunt Anna's husband, Stanislav Redens, had all been arrested, Uncle Pavel came to my father again and again to plead for colleagues of his in the army who'd been swallowed up in the giant wave. It never did any good. In the autumn of 1938, Pavel went to Sochi on vacation, and it was bad for his weak heart. When he got back he found that every one of his colleagues had disappeared. There had been so many arrests that it was as though the place had been swept by a broom. Pavel dropped dead of a heart attack in his office.

Beria, who was already in power in Moscow by this time, made up various stories about Pavel's death and kept trying to put them over on my father. The most farfetched was that Pavel had been poisoned by his wife. Heaven knows what else Beria managed to insinuate. But the plain fact was that the horror on all sides was too much for anybody's heart. Pavel was sensitive and reserved, just like my mother and grandfather. He kept the pain hidden inside until it finally killed him.

But that wasn't enough for Beria. A full decade later, in 1948, he had Pavel's widow accused of spying and poisoning her husband and she was thrown into jail. She and Anna Redens—Redens himself had been shot ten years before— were each given ten years' solitary confinement. Neither was set free until 1954.

My mother was closer to Pavel than to her older sister, Anna, but the two sisters were also very close. Their personalities differed but were not in conflict. Anna Redens is goodness itself, the very embodiment of the unfailing Christian spirit that forgives everything and everyone. I don't know anyone who has so unflaggingly devoted her whole life to other people, helping them, worrying about their troubles, always thinking of them first and herself last. Her attitude of Christian forbearance never failed to exasperate my father, who called her "an unprincipled fool" and remarked that "this sort of goodness is worse than any wickedness." My mother used to complain that "Anna spoils both her children and mine," because my aunt loved us all and was kind to us and overlooked the tricks little children play. It wasn't anything conscious or thought out on her part, but just the way she was. She couldn't be any other way.

Anna had once been very beautiful, slender as a reed, with features that were finely chiseled and regular, even more than my mother's, with warm brown eyes and magnificent teeth, like all the Alliluyev brothers and sisters. She had the same dark skin and slender hands, the same hint of the East in her looks. She married young and grew stout; like many people who have been beautiful all their lives, she couldn't have cared less about her looks. Unlike my neat and austere mother, she was always sloppily dressed. Her hair was held back with a round comb, and she paid no attention to appearances. She believed simply in doing good. To her the whole point of life was whether she would have a chance to perform some act of kindness or other. As for form and the externals, she didn't even give them a thought.

Her sister's lack of fastidiousness, the messiness and disorder of her home, jarred on my mother—in this they were opposites. But my mother loved her sister and was close to her. They both had the same outlook, one of profound humanity and faith in other people.

The running of the Redens household was left entirely to Tatyana, their splendid old nurse. She and my nurse were very close. Because of Tatyana, my aunt didn't have to worry about meals or the children. Aunt Anna worshiped her husband, Stanislav, a Polish Bolshevik and an old associate of Dzerzhinsky's. To her, he was and still is the best and most upstanding man who ever lived. I remember him only as very handsome, with a lively face and dazzling smile, and as being high-spirited and always kind to us children. They had two sons, both of them handsome in a way that was partly southern and partly Polish. They both grew up gentle and affectionate, like their mother, and good-looking, like their father.

People say Redens was tough, that he put on airs and wouldn't stand being contradicted. But I won't presume to judge what I don't remember and didn't see with my own eyes.

After the Civil War he was a leading Chekist in the Ukraine. He and his family lived in Kharkov. He was later transferred to the Georgian Cheka. This is where he first came into conflict with Beria, who was ambitious to become head of the Cheka in Georgia. They took an instant dislike to one another. Redens, after all, was a disciple of Dzerzhinsky's. Beria, on the other hand, thought of Georgia as his personal satrapy and a base for his future climb to power. Redens soon had to leave Georgia, and Beria entered on his reign as First Secretary of the Georgian Communist Party.

I shall come back later to Beria, who seems to have had a diabolic link with all our family and who wiped out a good half of its members. Olga Shatunovskaya, an Old Bolshevik from the Caucasus, who knew Beria's role and sized him up very early, is the one who told me about those days. But in fact all the old Party people in Transcaucasia knew him for exactly what he was. Had it not been for the inexplicable support of my father, whom Beria had cunningly won over, Kirov[3] and Ordzhonikidze and all the others who knew Transcaucasia and knew about the Civil War there would have blocked his advance. They, of course, were the very ones he destroyed first, as soon as he had a chance.

During the early 1930's Redens worked in the Cheka in Moscow. On account of his high position—he was a deputy to the first Supreme Soviet in 1936—my Aunt Anna didn't have to work or earn a living. But she was instinctively public-spirited. She spent all her time and energy on other people, helping them out and taking their children under her wing. Unlike the wives of other highly placed Chekists with all their foreign clothes, she was totally unacquisitive. She'd shrug off gossip with "My husband loves me just the way I am!" People were forever telling her that he was unfaithful. Who knows, maybe he was—he was no saint. But it never affected her in the slightest. Jealousy was a feeling that simply didn't exist for her. She would just laugh and say, "Oh, stop it. I love my husband and he loves me. What do I care if there's something else going on or not?" And it wasn't put on. She believed in him and in his feelings for her, as she believed in everyone.

Beria's appointment as head of the NKVD in Moscow

meant trouble for Redens, and he knew it. He had been assigned to the NKVD in Kazakhstan, and he and his family had left for Alma-Ata. They hadn't been there long when he was called back to Moscow. He came with a heavy heart, and was never seen again.

Toward the end he, like Uncle Pavel, tried to see my father to intercede for other people. My Aunt Anna said later that he and my father even had a quarrel; my father wouldn't tolerate the slightest attempt to change his mind about anybody. Once he had cast out of his heart someone he had known a long time, once he had mentally relegated that someone to the ranks of his enemies, it was impossible to talk to him about that person any more. He was constitutionally incapable of the reversal that would turn a fancied enemy back into a friend. Any effort to persuade him to do so only made him furious. No one—not Redens nor Uncle Pavel nor Alexander Svanidze—could get anywhere when it came to that kind of thing. The only thing they accomplished by it was loss of access to my father and total forfeiture of his trust. When he saw each of them for the last time, it was as if he were parting with someone who was no longer a friend, with someone, in fact, who was already an enemy.

Yet all of them were honorable men. They were all open, direct and honest with my father. None of them tried to play on his weaknesses—they had known him too long. They didn't try to deceive him—they thought it neither necessary nor possible. And each of them was the loser for it.

My Aunt Anna and her children came to Moscow after Redens was arrested. Unlike the wives of others who had vanished, she was allowed to keep her apartment. But she was no longer permitted to come to our house. Being only eleven at the time, I couldn't make out what had happened. Where had everybody gone? Why was the house so empty? The vague rumors to the effect that Uncle Stanislav was a bad man didn't make any sense. I merely became more and more aware how empty and deserted the house was and that I had nothing left but school and my kind nurse.

Aunt Anna refused to believe for a moment that her husband was a wicked, dishonest man and an enemy of the Soviet people. She refused to accept the fact that he had been shot, though my father was heartless enough to inform her of it in 1938 or '39. He thought he could force her to accept the idea that her husband had been what he called an enemy, but she couldn't conceive of such a thing. It was a matter of necessity to her to believe that he was alive and innocent and that he was coming back. And she believed it.

Grandmother and Grandfather did everything they could for her. She went on helping people and doing things for them exactly as before. To her friends' credit—they were old Party intellectuals, like her husband—every one of them stood by her. Not one of them turned away.

She was endowed in highest measure with the trustfulness and simplicity of spirit of the truly honorable person, one who is incapable of suspecting anyone else of wrongdoing because he is incapable of it himself. Often she'd say, "I'll go call on Voroshilov (or Kaganovich, or the Molotovs). He was so close to Stakh in the Ukraine."

And she'd go, though nobody else in her shoes would have dreamed of doing such a thing. She was quite right. They saw her and asked her to stay. They did their best to comfort her and spoke to her kindly and with warmth. Doors opened as if by magic before this short, ravaged, helpless woman, whose beauty was gone except for her warm brown eyes. She spoke gently and had no one to stand up for her. Indeed, everyone knew my father had repudiated her and would no longer have her in his house.

During the final years of the war she helped my grandfather with his memoirs. Someone suggested that she write her own memoirs, a schoolgirl's reminiscences of her own life and the Alliluyevs and the Revolution. She lacked the literary ability to do it herself. But she told it all to an editor named Nina Bam, who wrote it up into a book. I didn't find it very interesting. Grandfather's reminiscences, which he wrote himself, had plenty of personality. But Nina Bam's book was too contrived. It didn't do justice to my aunt, who was worthy of something better.

Nonetheless my father was outraged when the book came out in 1947. A devastating review appeared in *Pravda,* a review that was inadmissibly rude, shockingly unfair and dogmatic. The author was Fedoseyev,[4] but the more acid phrases can only have come from my father.

Everyone was frightened to death—everyone, that is, except Aunt Anna. She ignored the review for the simple reason that it was neither just nor true. She knew there was nothing to it. What more did she need? Nor was she afraid of my father. She knew him too well, after all. He was just another human being to her, subject to the usual human weaknesses and errors. Couldn't he be wrong, like anybody else? She just laughed and said she was working on the next volume.

But she never got the chance. In 1948, when a new wave of arrests swallowed and sent back to prison those who had already served ten-year sentences starting in 1937, not even my Aunt Anna was spared. She was arrested along with Academician Lina Shtern,[5] with Lozovsky,[6] and with Molotov's wife, Polina Zhemchuzhina,[7] an old and close friend of my mother's. She came back six years later in the spring of 1954. She had spent part of the time in solitary confinement, but mostly she'd been in the prison hospital. The curse of heredity—the schizophrenia that plagued my mother's family—had caught up with her. Even Aunt Anna failed to weather all the blows visited on her by fate.

She was in a terrible state. I saw her the first day she was back. She was sitting in her old room unable to recognize her two grown sons, oblivious of everyone. Her eyes were cloudy and she was staring out the window, indifferent to the news we were trying to tell her about my father's death, about Grandmother's death and the downfall of our sworn enemy, Beria. Her only reaction was to shake her head listlessly.

It's nine years since then, and Aunt Anna is somewhat better. Her mind no longer wanders. Sometimes she just talks to herself a little at night. Once again she's leading an active life as she did in the old days. She has been re-elected to the Union of Writers and goes to all the talks and meetings and lectures at the Writers' Club. She has quantities of old friends and acquaintances. Once again she tries to help everyone in sight. The day her pension arrives, myriad old ladies appear on her doorstep and she hands out money to them all, knowing perfectly well that none of them will ever be able to pay her back. People she's never seen in her life keep showing up at her apartment to ask for help. One wants a permit to stay in Moscow.[8] Another is looking for a job. An old schoolteacher has trouble at home and nowhere to live. Aunt Anna does what she can for all of them. She goes to the Moscow City Soviet. She spends hours waiting to see someone at the Presidium of the Supreme Soviet. She peppers the Central Committee with appeals, never for herself, of course, but for someone in trouble, some ailing old woman who doesn't have a pension and has nothing to live on.

She's a familiar figure everywhere she goes. Everybody respects her and is kind to her—everybody except her two young, good-looking daughters-in-law, who are out only for themselves. Her home life is terrible—no one consults her or pays her any attention. Sometimes they go to the movies and leave her to baby-sit. When they have friends in for the evening, she is an unwanted guest, a disheveled, white-haired old woman who is sloppily dressed and keeps butting in at the wrong moment. Instead of a purse, she'll pick up an old muff or sack and go out for a walk. She'll have a long talk with the militia-man on the street, ask the garbageman how he's been lately and go for a boat ride on the river. If this were before the Revolution, people would treat her like a holy woman and bow down before her on the street.

Life plays tricks on us all. After she finished school, Aunt Anna started neuropsychiatric training in St. Petersburg. She'd have been a splendid psychiatrist, understanding and compassionate. But her life worked out differently and she became a mental patient instead.

For years now she's been waging a campaign for our apartment house* to have its own kindergarten. There are five hundred apartments in the building. Many of the children have maids to look after them, but by no means all. Aunt Anna has appealed to countless officials. Although she has heart trouble, emphysema and a weak lung as a result of an early bout of tuberculosis, she gives freely of her time and strength. So far she hasn't succeeded. They always decide that we don't need a kindergarten or even a playground in our courtyard, which is as dark as a stone-lined pit.

She is a missionary of good, a saint and a perfect Christian, but she is also the spirit of the future. She is a true daughter of Russia, a classic Russian type, straight out of Dostoyevsky. She never judges or condemns. She's beside herself when people talk about the "cult of personality." She gets worked up and talks on and on. "They're exaggerating. They always exaggerate in this country," she'll say indignantly. "Now they're blaming everything on Stalin. But he didn't have an easy time either. We know his life wasn't easy. It wasn't as simple as all that. Think of all the time he spent in Siberia. We mustn't

* The so-called government house, near the Kamenny Bridge.

forget that. And we mustn't forget the good things he did!"

She's convinced her husband is still alive, although she's had official word of his posthumous rehabilitation. She thinks he has a new wife and family somewhere in the Far North like Kolyma or Magadan ("After so many years, why not?" she'll ask) and that he just doesn't want to come home. From time to time she'll insist after one of her dreams or hallucinations that she's seen her husband and had a talk with him.

She lives in a world of her own, where memories and visions and shadows of bygone years blur into those of the present. The six years she spent in prison are the one thing she never talks about. She only remembers the pleasant, interesting things and the wonderful people—and she knew a good many of those.

She spent a long time trying to persuade me to write down everything I could remember. I was stubborn and turned a deaf ear. I thought that what I wrote would be no good and that it would be an embarrassing, tactless, even cheap thing to do. You made me change my mind, my friend. You talked me into it, and now I can't tear myself away from what I'm writing. And now, even for me, everything I knew is turning into something meaningful and important.*

The story of my mother's brothers won't be complete until I say something about Fyodor. He, too, shared the family fate. Only, life destroyed him a bit sooner than the others.

He was brilliant at physics, mathematics and chemistry. He was so gifted that just before the Revolution he was accepted in the school for the aristocratic Marine Guards. Then came the Revolution and Civil War. Of course he went into

---

* Anna Redens died in August, 1964, in a section of the Kremlin hospital located outside Moscow. After prison she had a great fear of locked doors, but despite her protests she was locked up one night in a hospital ward. The next morning she was found dead.

the army. He was assigned to intelligence. Kamo[9] wanted him, the daring, legendary Kamo, who'd known the family in Tiflis. But this time Kamo was wrong. By no means everyone could bear what Kamo and his men with their nerves of iron could stand without batting an eye. He had a way of putting his men's loyalty to the test. One time he staged a mock raid in which it was made to look as if the whole of their unit had been smashed and all the men seized and bound, while on the floor lay the bloody corpse of their commander with his heart torn out and lying on the ground. The object of the test was to see what the raw recruit would do once he'd been taken prisoner. How would he handle himself?

Uncle Fyodor didn't pass the test. One look at the chaos and blood and he went right out of his mind. He never got over it. He was a semi-invalid for the rest of his life, a kind, clever man who devoured every book he could get his hands on and wrote countless treatises, articles and plays. He lived on a pension and died at about the age of sixty never having done anything with his life at all. All he had, his life, his youth, his talent and his health, he gave to the Revolution. Probably he ought to have been a scholar or scientist. That's what he was cut out for, and he could have been far more help to the Revolution that way than with Kamo and his cutthroats.

I hardly knew Uncle Fyodor and saw him only a few times. He was very fond of my mother and he loved us because we were her children. But his illness made him solitary and shy. It took everything out of him, even the capacity to have a family. Unlike his brother and sisters, he was unprepossessing to look at. The only thing about him was his wonderful eyes. They were warm and brown and ever so gentle. He was slovenly and badly dressed and he slopped up his food at the table. Like many people who are mentally ill, he was repellent to strangers. But friends and relations knew the value of his goodness and his learning. My father was sorry for him. But he avoided him and made fun of his eccentricities.

All the Alliluyev children were too thin-skinned, sensitive and generous to come through this fearful life unscathed. All of them were talented and had it in them to lead worthwhile lives. But not one of them managed to live his life to its natural end. Not one had a quiet, constructive existence. Not one tried to live a comfortable life or be "happy" in a conventional way.

I still haven't told you about my mother. I promise to, but it will be very hard. If you'll wait a little, I'll tell you about her later. It's my mother I've been talking about all this time, after all. Don't you see her next to Grandfather and Grandmother, next to Anna and Pavel and Fyodor? Don't you see how close they were and how very much alike? Don't you see what kindred spirits all of them were?

I keep trying to bring back what is gone, the sunny, bygone years of my childhood. That's why I want to tell you about everybody who was part of our life in the Kremlin and at Zubalovo. I still have to tell you about Alexander Svanidze, the brother of my father's first wife, and his wife Maria, since both of them were extremely close to my father and to my mother as well.

⇛ 6

You have already seen that to all our family Georgia was alive, was its native soil. To all of them, to my mother and grandparents, Georgia, with its abundance of sunshine, its strong emotions, its love of beauty and the inborn grace of its princes and peasants alike, was the wonderful place celebrated by the poets of Russia. It wasn't because my father was born there that Georgia was a living presence in our house. He was the one, I think, who cared about it least. It was Russia that he loved. He loved Siberia, with its stark beauty and its rough, silent people. He hated the feudal homage the Georgians paid him. He thought about Georgia only when he was an old man.

Maybe the love they all had for Georgia has something to do with the fact that the relatives of my father's first wife, Yekaterina Svanidze, were so close to my mother and her family.

Or maybe it was the fact that my mother had the knack of making them all feel at home in my father's house—or, rather, her house, the house of which she was the mistress and where my father was just a presence forever weighted down by political quarrels and disagreements.

But today I don't feel like writing about the past. The life of today, the life that's seething and glittering all around, crowds in on all sides, not letting me bury myself in the past. It's carrying me in another direction altogether.

My son has left for physics class in Moscow. He wants to go to the medical institute and is getting ready for the examinations. It's strange that of his eight grandchildren my father saw only three—my two children and Yakov's daughter—and that, although he always was cold and unfair to Yakov, he felt real tenderness for Yakov's daughter, Gulia. It's stranger still that he also displayed love and tenderness toward my son, the son of my first husband, a Jew and a man my father refused to meet even once.

I'll never forget how scared I was the first time my father saw my son Josef. He was about three and very appealing, a little Greek- or Georgian-looking, with huge, shiny Jewish eyes and long lashes. I was sure my father wouldn't approve; I didn't see how he possibly could. But I know nothing about the vagaries of the human heart, I guess. My father melted the moment he set eyes on the child.

It was in 1949, on one of the very few visits he made after the war to Zubalovo, which was deserted by now, quiet and sad beyond all recognition. There were only three people living in the place: Josef, his nurse, and my old nurse, who was ill by this time. I was in my last year at the university, living in Moscow. The child was growing up in the care of the two gentle old ladies and under the pine tree that by tradition was mine. My father played with Josef half an hour, wandered, or rather ran, outside the house—he had the brisk step of a young man till his dying day—and went away. I stayed behind reliving that half-hour and going over everything that had happened in my mind.

I was in seventh heaven. With a man of few words like my father, his "He's a good-looking boy—he's got nice eyes" was like a paean of praise from anybody else. I realized that I had no understanding of life and its many surprises. He saw Josef twice more. The last time was four months before he died. Josef was seven and had just started the first grade. "What thoughtful eyes," my father said again. "He's a smart boy!" And again I was overjoyed.

Strangely enough, Josef, too, remembers this last meeting with his grandfather and how well they hit it off. Unpolitical though he is—he's like the rest of his generation—he ought all the same to hate everything associated with the "cult of personality," everything that's been attributed to one man, and this man in particular. In fact, he does hate the cult and all its associations, but he doesn't make any connection between them and his grandfather. He put his grandfather's picture on his desk a long time ago and it's there still. I make no effort to interfere. You have to trust children. This again makes me feel that I don't understand life and all its surprises.

My son is eighteen now. He's finished school, and of all the professions he might have chosen he has picked the most humanitarian, that of doctor. I'm very glad—so glad, in fact, that I'm afraid of showing it for fear he might reconsider.

He is gentle, handsome, affectionate. My daughter and her best friend are playing in the woods. It's one of nature's mistakes that they are girls; they ought to have been a pair of boys. They climb trees and fences. They race each other on bicycles and go swimming in the river. At night they camp out in tents. They teach dogs and cats to do tricks and they play basketball. Neither one of my children knows, or needs to know, how much I love being near them, or the fact that it is they who are teaching me about life and not I who am teaching them. How happy I am that my children are growing up in the same woods I grew up in, breathing the same air from the same sweet-smelling fields and meadows, and that maybe they'll think of Zhukovka as their home and the place they belong for the rest of their life, as I do.

As for my daughter Katya (Yekaterina), my father was fond of her father, who was my second husband, and liked the entire Zhdanov family. Yet he wasn't especially fond of our daughter. He only saw her once, when she was two and a half. She was funny as a button, with pink cheeks and dark eyes that were big as cherries. He took one look at her and burst out laughing. The rest of the evening he never stopped laughing.

It was November 8, 1952, the twentieth anniversary of my mother's death. We never mentioned the anniversary, and I've no idea whether my father even knew what day it was. But of course I couldn't forget it. So I took the children and the three of us went to the *dacha*. It wasn't easy to bring off, as I had trouble getting to see my father at all during his final years.

It was the next to the last time I saw him—four months before he died. I think he enjoyed it. The table was piled high with good things to eat, fresh fruit and vegetables and nuts. There was good Georgian wine, the real thing, straight from the countryside and served in tiny glasses. My father knew all the best Georgian wines and during his last years had them shipped to him specially. He always insisted on having an enormous selection, practically a battery of bottles, on the table, even though he himself might not touch them.

Though he didn't eat much either and only picked at things here and there, he insisted on having an abundant selection on the table. That was his rule. On this occasion the children feasted on fruit, and he was pleased. He liked sitting at the table watching other people eat.

Why am I thinking of this particular evening all of a sudden? Because it was the first and only time my father and the two children and I were all together. It was nice the way he had wine served to the children in the fashion of the Caucasus. Luckily, they didn't act finicky or refuse. They behaved perfectly and everyone was happy. Did my father wish we were all living under the same roof? Would he have liked it? Probably he would. But he was tired by then. He was used to the freedom of being lonely. He and I had led such separate lives those last twenty years that we could never have created a single household, the semblance of a family, a shared existence, even if we both wanted to. He really didn't want to, I guess. But we all have that evening to remember, even the children.

We are sitting out on the porch. My son is boning up on physics; my daughter is deep in a science fiction novel; Mishka the cat is purring. It's hot and still. The woods around us are buzzing with wasps and bees. The linden is in bloom. It's a quiet, wilting heat. Nature is peaceful, beautiful, perfect. It is engaged in its usual round, oblivious of everything.

O Lord, how lovely is this earth of yours and how perfect, every blade of grass, every flower and leaf! And You go on supporting man and giving him strength in this fearful bedlam where Nature alone, invincible and eternal, gives solace and strength, harmony and tranquillity of spirit.

Only those whom God has cursed and abandoned can bear to violate the beauty and majesty of earth or think of destroying what grows and blossoms and makes life joyful. What a terrible thing that there are so many madmen in the world! What a terrible thing, and how wrong, that they set aims for themselves and for the sake of these aims consider the destruction of life itself to be justified!

To the poorest peasant woman it is plain that such a thing cannot be allowed to happen. Yet men and women who claim to be civilized fail to see it. The Chinese Communists, who claim to be Marxists, believe that it is not merely feasible but necessary for human beings to destroy one another.

Evil and insanity are on one side of the scale; intelligence, progress, brotherhood and humaneness on the other. World peace hangs in this hellish balance. So do we, our generation, our children, the era itself. We must all of us have faith in the power of decency and goodwill.

It seems to me that in our time faith in God is the same thing as faith in good and the ultimate triumph of good over evil. Religious differences no longer have any meaning in the world today, where men and women of reason, intelligence and compassion have already attained an understanding of one another that transcends the boundaries between countries and continents, races and tongues.

Dogmatic differences between religions are losing their importance. It's simpler to divide people today into believers and unbelievers. By the time I was thirty-five and had seen something of life, I, who'd been taught from earliest childhood by society and my family to be an atheist and materialist, was already one of those who cannot live without God. I am glad that it is so.

I'd like to tell you more about Alexander Svanidze, the brother of my father's first wife. He was three years younger than my father and one of the early Georgian Bolsheviks. He had been called "Alyosha" in the underground, and later on the name stuck. Even we children called him "Uncle Alyosha." Thanks to my mother, he and his wife Maria were very close to us and to all my mother's family. They were a remarkable couple.

Uncle Alexander was handsome in the way that people from the mountain region of Svanetia are. He was blond and blue-eyed, with a thin, aquiline nose. He was stocky and not very tall. He was well dressed to the point of being a dandy. Georgians are extremely sensitive about their appearance and have the knack of looking well without any apparent effort. Their

Marxist convictions are no obstacle whatever. As for my Uncle Alexander, not only was he an educated Marxist of the old school, but he had a European background besides. Before the Revolution the Party sent him to the University at Jena, Germany. He knew Oriental as well as European languages, and he was expert in history, economics and, above all, finance. When World War I broke out he was in Germany and was immediately interned. The Germans released him after the Revolution and he returned to his native Georgia. He quickly became the first People's Commissar of Finance and a member of the Party Central Committee there. He also married my Aunt Maria, who came from a well-to-do family. She had been educated in St. Petersburg and at the music conservatory in Tiflis and was a singer with the Tiflis opera.

Aunt Maria was very beautiful. She was from a wealthy Jewish family, the Koronas, who were of Spanish extraction, yet her features were more Slavic than anything else. Her face was oval, and she had a tiny, turned-up nose, peaches-and-cream coloring and huge blue eyes. She was a big woman, good-natured and well dressed, and she always wore good perfume. They were a splendid pair, and they both charmed everyone in sight.

Do you think it odd that I talk all the time about everybody's being beautiful or handsome? It was a different age—people really were good-looking then. Just look at the old Russian revolutionaries. They all had marvelous faces, eyes that were full of expression, firm lips and high, intellectual foreheads. There were no doubts, no skepticism, no meanness in their faces.

Uncle Alexander never had a career in politics or the Party. I've no idea whether that's how he wanted it or not. In any case he devoted himself wholly to finance. The new government sent him abroad early, and he and his family lived in Berlin before the rise of Hitler, and later in Geneva and London. He came back to Moscow and was head of the Bank for Foreign Trade up to 1937. During this latter period and before, while my mother was still alive, the Svanidzes were at our house all the time.

I believe my mother loved them, and I know they loved her. Both of them were a good deal older than she, and they were extremely affectionate to her and to us children. Aunt Maria was forever trying to brighten my mother's rather Spartan life and was always bringing presents to all of us from Berlin.

Both husband and wife were European in the very best sense of the word. Whenever I see the petty, narrow-minded nationalism of Georgians nowadays and hear them tactlessly speaking Georgian in front of those who don't understand, hear them praising everything Georgian to the skies and running down everything else, I can't help thinking how different people were in the old days. They couldn't have cared less about this hateful "national question"! People were friendly and they trusted one another then. They didn't give a hang about acquiring country houses and furniture and cars.

Aunt Maria had been trained in economics in St. Peters burg before the Revolution. When she and her husband were abroad and afterward, when they were back in Moscow, she gave her husband first-rate advice in economic matters. She was in on all his decisions and knew everything about his work and the people he was seeing.

I remember their coming to Zubalovo. They lived in a wing of Zubalovo Two and they'd come over to our house on foot. Zubalovo Two was always full of people, a revolving vacation retreat. Mikoyan's sons, Gamarnik's[1] daughter, and the sons and daughters of Voroshilov and Shaposhnikov all have memories of this happy, hospitable place. They had movies there, silent ones and occasionally talkies. There was a tennis court

for children and adults to play on. There was even a Russian
bath for those who liked it, including my father. The Svanidzes
had a son with the peculiar name of Johnreed, in honor of the
famous American journalist.[2] When he was little we all called
him Johnny or Johnik, but now he's Ivan Alexandrovich. He
has the same happy memories of their house at Zubalovo as I
have of ours.

The Svanidzes had become parents rather late in life and
adored little Johnik. They taught him all they conceivably
could. Since German was the fashion in those days, not English, as it is today, they had him tutored in German. They also
had him taught music, clay modeling and drawing. He started
writing poetry at the age of five and compiled books of verse
in a large, childish script. Uncle Alexander had ideas about
Johnik's upbringing that differed from those of Lidia
Trofimovna, the governess and nurse. Once he found out that
Johnik had shoved his kitten into the fireplace and singed it.
Uncle Alexander gave a loud curse. He grabbed his son by the
hand, dragged him to the fireplace and thrust his hand into the
flames. The little boy howled with pain. My uncle then told
him that "It hurt kitty, too!" He stood up for what he considered to be right with true Georgian spirit.

He loved his son dearly and on Sundays used to take him
walking in the woods outside the *dacha*. During their walks
he used to tell him about history, which he knew and loved,
especially ancient history, stories about Persians and Hittites
and Greeks. Toward the end of his life he wrote articles for
the *Ancient History Journal* on the origin of the tribes of
ancient Georgia. He was expert in Georgian poetry and did a
good deal of work on the texts of the poet Rustaveli.

Aunt Maria didn't spend so much time with her son. She
spoiled him and turned him over wholly to the governess. In
Moscow she had given up opera singing, but she often took
part in concerts. She enjoyed social life and had a talent for

it. She had good taste and a large and hospitable house that was filled with objects of beauty and value. I remember both of them, especially Aunt Maria, as being high-spirited, kind and very affectionate to me. I used to throw myself on Uncle Alexander's neck and refuse to get off his lap.

My father loved both of them, especially Uncle Alexander, and treated them like real members of the family. Did they have their differences when it came to politics? Were there political disagreements between my father and Uncle Alexander or Redens or Uncle Pavel? Maybe. People weren't afraid of having their own opinions in those days, and they had them on every subject. They were unafraid of life and refused to close their eyes to its complexities. But I don't know the facts. The one thing I do know is that they weren't just relatives but were very close to my father, and that their words and ideas and the information they brought him about the real world —from which he was already isolated—were tremendously important to him. I'm sure he trusted them then. I'm sure it never entered his head to suspect them of being covert "enemies of the people" or personal enemies of his, two things that later, unfortunately, came to mean one and the same thing.

They kept on coming to see us after my mother died, though there was no longer any lady of the house and her welcoming spirit was gone. They came to our house at Zubalovo for Vasily's and my birthdays. Once the grownups put on a puppet show for us—*Othello*. Aunt Maria and my other aunts pushed the sofa away from the wall and with the help of my poor puppets put on the tragedy, which turned out to be very funny indeed. Afterward Aunt Maria sang. We children weren't interested and didn't listen.

Redens was arrested in 1937. That was the first blow. Soon afterward both the Svanidzes were arrested.

How could such a thing happen? How could my father do

it? The only thing I know is that it couldn't have been his idea. But if a skillful flatterer, like Beria, whispered slyly in his ear that "these people are against you," that there were "compromising material" and "dangerous connections," such as trips abroad, my father was capable of believing it. I'll tell you later how shattered he was by the death of both my mother and Kirov. Maybe he never trusted people very much, but after their deaths stopped trusting them at all. His opinion of people could be manipulated. It became possible to insinuate that so-and-so had turned out to be "no good." Even though he'd been well thought of for years, he merely seemed to be all right. "Actually, he's an enemy. He's been saying bad things about you; he opposes you. X, Y and Z have given evidence against him." What my father didn't want to realize was that in the cellars of the secret police X, Y and Z could be made to testify to anything. That was the domain of Beria, Yezhov[3] and the other executioners, whom nature had endowed with a special talent for that sort of thing.

And when the "facts" convinced my father that someone he knew well had turned out "badly" after all, a psychological metamorphosis came over him. Maybe in his heart of hearts he still had his doubts, and wondered and suffered over it. But he was in the grip of an iron logic whereby once you've said A, then B and C have to follow. Once he accepted the premise that X was his enemy, the premise became axiomatic, and no matter what the facts might be, they had to be made to fit. My father was psychologically unable ever to go back to believing that X wasn't an enemy but an honest man after all.

At this point—and this was where his cruel, implacable nature showed itself—the past ceased to exist for him. Years of friendship and fighting side by side in a common cause might as well never have been. Difficult as it is to understand, he could wipe it all out at a stroke—and X would be doomed.

"So you've betrayed me," some inner demon would whisper.
"I don't even know you any more." Remembering his old attitude toward them, men and women he'd worked with for
years, colleagues and friends of long standing, might plead
with him, but it was all in vain. He was deaf to them already.
He couldn't go back. He couldn't even remember. In his cold-
blooded way, he cared about only one thing: How is X con-
ducting himself now? Does he admit his mistakes?

My father was astonishingly helpless before Beria's machinations. All Beria had to do was bring him the record of the
interrogation in which X "confessed," or others "confessed"
for him or, worse yet, X refused to "confess."

As Khrushchev mentioned at the Twenty-second Party Congress,[4] Uncle Alexander held out. He refused to "confess" or
"ask forgiveness." He refused, in other words, to write letters
appealing to my father as many others did, always to no avail.
Uncle Alexander had the courage and strength of a real Bolshevik. It was in keeping with his splendid character. But he
paid for his courage and dignity and restraint. He was shot in
February, 1942, at the age of sixty.

That was during the war. He was in a prison camp outside
Ukhta,[5] to which he had been sent for an indefinite term.
After their arrest and investigation, he and Aunt Maria each
got ten years, but she was sent to a different place, to Dolin-
skoye, a women's prison camp in Kazakhstan. Yet sentences
of this kind meant nothing. In 1942 a great many people in
camps were shot, though they might have been sentenced only
to exile, hard labor and long prison terms. I've no idea why
this happened, whether it was the way the war was going—
it was still going badly and victory hadn't yet been won at
Stalingrad—or whether Beria had simply made up his mind
to get rid of those who knew about his crimes and had no trouble talking my father into it.

When the sentence that had been carried out against Uncle

Alexander was read to my Aunt Maria, she dropped dead of a heart attack.

It was only during the war, when they were both in prison camps, he in the north and she in the south, that they had finally been given permission to write to their son, Johnik, who was living in Moscow with his nurse. She literally saved his life. She took him in and shared with him what little food she could buy on her earnings in a Moscow clothing factory.

I didn't see Johnik after 1937. We met again, twenty-five years later, and he showed me his letters from his parents and told me all he knew of what had happened to them. They contained the usual affectionate questions a parent asks a child. How were things at school? Was he in good health? Was everything all right? Each one expressed the hope that the boy's many relatives were looking out for him. They said it many times over. But the fact is, the relatives refused. My brother Yakov wanted to take him in, but his wife begged him not to. She said Johnik was difficult and spoiled, and, besides, he had uncles and aunts of his own. But Uncle Alexander's sister Mariko had been arrested, too, and soon died in prison. Aunt Maria's brother, whom she'd counted on to look out for Johnik, was also in prison, though he was lucky enough to survive and is still alive today.

The only one left was Lidia, his nurse, a religious old maid who worshiped Uncle Alexander and considered it her sacred duty to bring the child up just as long as she had the strength. She did everything she could.

The dreadful change in his parents' fortunes hurled Johnik from the summit of luxury to the very bottom: later on he was imprisoned with common criminals, and then exiled to Kazakhstan. In spite of this, and in spite of a congenital nervous condition, he grew up worthy of his remarkable father and mother. Everything they managed to teach him in their eleven happy years together stood him in good stead later on. In 1956 he was finally admitted to Moscow University to study history. He got nothing but A's. He had no difficulty getting through graduate school and obtaining his doctor's degree at the Institute of African Studies. He had inherited his parents' tremendous ability.

The only thing that didn't stand up was his health—his nerves frequently give out. Intimates find him hard to get along with. But others who aren't so close, like his colleagues at the Institute and the voters of his district who elected him a deputy of the local soviet, consider him goodhearted, honest and sympathetic. He is disinterested and wants nothing for himself. But when, say, he's on the warpath to get a one-room apartment for some poor family in a basement, he could strangle anyone who stands in the way with his own hands. Though he was born in Berlin in 1926 and has never been to Georgia in his life, he has the hot-blooded Georgian temperament and inability to compromise.

These are the people who made up our household. This is the cast of characters I remember from my childhood.

A terrible destiny awaited each one of them. Each died a different death. But death came inexorably to them all.

Uncle Alexander and Aunt Maria had both led long and useful lives when they died past the age of fifty. But my mother, Redens and Uncle Pavel died young and didn't have time to make so much of their lives. Aunt Anna and Uncle Fyodor became invalids, and so life, in a sense, was taken from them. My grandparents lived to be nearly eighty. But after my mother died, their life was one long agony because of all that was going on around them.

These men and women had once been a boisterous, happy family. All that remains of this are the snapshots taken in the garden and on the terrace at Zubalovo and in Sochi, where all of us used to go in the summer. And there are the children—Uncle Pavel's daughter and two sons, the two sons of Anna Redens, Ivan Svanidze and I—and we have our memories. Each of us has something in his heart to treasure. Each has a collection of faded snapshots with its happy, smiling faces.

I spent nearly seven years in a normal, happy family and it gave each of us a good deal. The household revolved around the children. It was my mother's rule and her law.

⇻ 8

Well, my friend, no matter how I try to put it off, the time has come when I have to tell you about my mother, though probably you already see what kind of person she was. There are a lot of legends about her, some of them false, romantic or absurd and others that are downright hostile.

My mother's life was as clear as crystal. Her character was all of a piece, the kind that carries conviction. She was true to it all her short life.

Some say my mother was a saint, others that she was mentally unbalanced. Neither of these things is true, any more than the story that she was murdered.

Luckily I have some of her letters. They'll give you a good idea of what she was like. Aunt Anna recently gave me copies of my mother's letters to A. I. and I. I. Radchenko,[1] close friends of my grandparents. They begin in 1916 and go up to 1924. They start out as the letters of a schoolgirl and show her growing up under our very eyes. I think they're worth giving in full.

My mother was born in Baku and her childhood was spent in the Caucasus. Because of her southern looks, people who didn't know Georgia sometimes took her for a Georgian. Actually, she had the looks of a southern Slav. She had the oval face, dark eyebrows, slightly turned-up nose, dark skin, soft brown eyes and straight black lashes that one sees in women from Greece or Bulgaria or the Ukraine. She also had something of the Gypsy about her, something languid and Oriental, sad eyes and long, slender fingers. She liked wearing shawls and they were becoming to her. She'd have looked well in an Indian sari.

She was the youngest of the family. Her sister and two brothers loved her and spoiled her. It is a happy, well-behaved, affectionate girl of fifteen we see in her early letters to the Radchenkos.

May 1, 1916

DEAR ALISA IVANOVNA,

Forgive me for taking so long to answer your letter, but I haven't had time. I was such a lazy-bones last summer that I had to spend ten full days studying for examinations. I had to catch up in algebra and geometry. I took my exams this morning and I don't know whether I passed. I think I passed everything but Russian composition. Our assigned topic was easy, but it's one of my weakest subjects.

I'm going to a new school because the old one is moving away. My new school is opposite Nicolaevsky Station.

Thank you for the pictures, dear Alisa Ivanovna. Nyura (Anna) and I had our pictures taken, too. Nyura's is ready, but mine isn't done yet. Nyura is about to go to the Neuropsychiatric Institute, but classes haven't begun yet. There is a preparatory school in our apartment house. One of the teachers is sick and Nyura is substituting for her.

The next letter is dated September 10, 1916, and was written to Alisa Ivanovna and her little boy Alyosha, or Nyaka.

I'm at my new school already. It wasn't hard switching, but I haven't made any friends. I'm still getting used to it. The other girls are all right, but they don't like newcomers. They're not specially nice to me because I'm new. I think it'll all straighten out in time.

Nyura's been accepted at the Psychiatric Institute. We'd like to know where Ivan Ivanovich is now. How is he, and is he coming here soon? We'd like very much to see him. There's not much to draw him here, I'm afraid. We get up and go to bed early. I'm yawning already, yet it's only eight at night. We're up with the roosters and asleep with the hens. How's Nyaka? Is he well and do he and Lida play? I'd like to know how all of you are and how you're getting on with the garden. Nyura and Fedya have two pupils. One is a girl in the fourth class and the other is a boy in the second. . . .

We think Pavlusha's going to be sent to Pskov or Archangel. He's just been home to get his things. He says he's going. It's a little too bad because he's not in very good health. We haven't any other news. I send you my very best. I kiss you warmly. Everyone in our house sends their best.

The next two letters were written in December, 1916. The family was still worried about Pavel's going into the army and the fact that Fyodor might have to go too.

We'll be out on vacation soon. I think we're spending Christmas in Petrograd. It takes too long to go anywhere and, besides, it's difficult and expensive. I like school, though I'm not quite at home there yet.

I suppose Nyaka will have a Christmas tree. Tell him to have a good time and not to get sick over New Year's. My best to him and to you. Everyone at our house sends regards.

And ten days later:

Our three weeks' vacation has begun. I'm going to sleep a lot, though we have a lot of homework, especially history and Russian. They gave us our marks for the second quarter. Everything came out all right. I had a lot of threes,[2] but luckily no twos. I have the hardest time with German because we're supposed to learn sight reading and not translation. I don't know German at all, or French either for that matter. I finally got a five in Bible. That was unheard of for me, but I worked at it very hard all quarter. I'm glad I changed schools. The girls are very nice and I like them very much. I miss them already, though it's only been one day. . . .

As you know, my oldest brother is in Novgorod. Mama and Papa are just managing as usual. I've been keeping a diary over a month now, and it keeps me very busy. When I have no one to talk to, I put down what I've got to say there. I'm glad I started it, though maybe I'll get tired of it soon. I hope you and Nyaka are better and that you start a good new life in New Year. . . .

In January, 1917, she wrote:

Tomorrow I'm staying home from school on account of the cold. I just got back from my music lesson nearly frozen. I took the exam on the third of January and got a five! I'm very pleased. It was hard taking music too, but I couldn't bear to give it up. I hope you're better by now and that Nyaka is going tobogganing and skating. Meantime we're in something boring like Bible when I'd rather be out enjoying the weather. Nyura's at her Psychiatric Institute, too, learning Latin. She sends her apologies for not writing.

I can hardly wait for summer. Alisa Ivanovna, I had an idea I want to ask you about. Mama and Nyura and I have been wondering where we'll go. I said what I wanted and Mama agreed. Now the question is whether you agree, too. I want to come and work at the Electric Station. I'm almost sixteen and I'm old enough to work now. I'd like to stay with you. Please let me know whether or not you approve. Nyura's going to stay with some friends near the Black Sea. Mama's going to take three weeks' vacation because she's very tired and thin. Besides she's been very upset ever since Pavel left. He'll probably be sent to the front in a month. They gave him three inoculations simultaneously.

Here is a letter of February 27, 1917, on the eve of the Revolution:

I've finally gotten around to writing you. I've been terribly busy all this time. But now school's closed for the fourth straight day because Petrograd is so unsettled, so I have some free time. It's very, very tense here. I wonder what it's like in Moscow. Practically nobody's home. Nyura is at Mama's brother's, Fedya is staying somewhere else too, Papa is in town, and Mama and I are sitting up waiting for Papa—he's very late for some reason.

We've had very little school since Christmas. First it was cold and then I was sick and now you can't go out on the street. I'd say more about what's going on, but I don't think it's a good idea to say too much in a letter. I'm going to spend the next few days reading Chekhov so as not to be too bored. I'm sick of winter and can hardly wait for the hot summer weather. It's been a very cold winter and I don't suppose Nyaka has been playing outside a lot. My very best wishes and I kiss you warmly.

The same day, February 27, she also sent a postcard.

We've all been fed up because for four days now there's been no way of getting around Petrograd. But now a great day has come, the twenty-seventh of February! Papa and I are the only ones at home—the others have all gone into town on foot. Nyura isn't well. She's been in bed at Uncle's for five days and hasn't been home, but Fedya looks in from time to time. Papa's very excited and stays by the telephone the whole time. Abel Yenukidze arrived today at the Nicolaevsky Station. To his surprise, he was in time for all the celebrations. All the best.

Love,

NADYA

What they were celebrating was the February Revolution. Grandfather came home and told everyone what was going on. Still nobody understood, but then Yenukidze appeared straight from exile in Siberia! Uncle Abel was my mother's godfather. The whole family knew him and loved him and had been sending him packages in Siberia. My father was also in exile at this time and used to write to Grandmother from Siberia. The family sent him packages there, too, as he was an old friend and a comrade in the cause all of them shared.

A letter dated March 30 shows that my mother was gradually beginning to notice the events going on around her, though school was still the main thing in her life.

A lot has happened in this short time. Did you hear that Chkheidze's[3] son died unexpectedly? I saw Chkheidze at the funeral. He looked ever so sad. In spite of it he's just as active as ever. I feel terribly sorry for him.

On March 13 we went to the funeral of all the people who were killed. It was very impressive, though we had to spend seven hours standing in one place. We were singing the whole time, however, and hardly noticed how long it was. We were struck by how beautiful the Field of Mars[4] was when we got there in the evening. There were torches and music. It was altogether a dazzling sight. We got home tired and wet, but we were in good spirits somehow and were feeling uplifted. Papa was one of the marshals. He wore a red sash and carried a white flag in his hand.

Thank you for your invitation. My work at school has been going slowly because we've all been so busy with other things. We have exams in botany and zoology after Easter, so I'll have to get down to work. They say school will be over by May 20, but that those of us in the middle grades will be out by the fifteenth. We're angry because delegates were elected from the sixth, seventh and eighth grades but they told us we were too young and stupid. But we have our own study circle and we're working very hard. We're starting a library. We help one another in the harder subjects, and are trying to make the class into a friendly, united whole. Unfortunately there are too many children in our class who are simply a nuisance. We had a meeting that

lasted three and a half hours not long ago. I am quite active and
go nearly every time. I'm the treasurer, though I haven't had
any experience and don't know how to do it very well. They're
pleased with me just the same.

Holiday greetings to all of you.

My mother spent July and August, 1917, at the Radchenkos'
dacha. Grandfather was busy in the Party. Lenin spent several days in July hiding out in the Alliluyevs' apartment,
where he was put in my mother's little room. The apartment
is now a museum. The walls are covered with pictures that
were taken then, and the things that were in my mother's
room at that time are still there: a rug, a narrow iron cot, a
dresser and a table.

I was in Leningrad in the summer of 1955 for the first time
and went to see my grandparents' apartment. It felt uncanny
to be on the same stairs my mother used to run down on her
way to school. And it was strange being in the apartment
where she first met my father. Luckily there were no other
visitors, so I spent a long time roaming through the empty
rooms and lingering in the kitchen trying to imagine what
their life was like.

It was all strange, but the strangest thing of all is that it
didn't make me the least bit sad. Although it's an official
place now and has the look of a museum, I felt a breath of
family warmth and love. There was still something vital and
alive in the air. I could feel my mother's spirit and sense that
it never left this cozy place at all, that it never really lived in
the Kremlin and couldn't stand being there. The Kremlin
never was the place for her. Those formal apartments and the
life she had to lead after she left here—all of it was alien to
her. It wasn't her kind of life. Here she was and still is
a pretty schoolgirl, learning her first history lessons not from
books but from the life around her. This was her home, the

home of her parents and family. It was her city. They should never have left. Maybe then the fate of the entire family would have been quite different and much happier.

In the autumn of 1917 my mother and her family were all in Petrograd again. On October 19 she wrote another letter to Alisa Radchenko.

I have a lot of work now, and two extra hours of music every day. It's past eleven already, and I still haven't done my French. I never go to bed before one. The others all go to bed, but I stay up doing my homework.

We've no plans for leaving the city. It's still possible to get food. Milk, bread, meat and eggs are all available, though costly. People are managing somehow, though we and everybody else are in an awful frame of mind. Sometimes it makes you cry. It's so dull, and you can't go anywhere. Actually, my music teacher did take me a few days ago to hear *Sorochinsk Fair* at the Musical Drama Theater and it was very good. There are rumors going around that the Bolsheviks are going to do something on October 20, but probably there's nothing to it. Well, all the best to you for the time being. I'll write Nyaka as soon as I have time. Meanwhile please tell him I thank him very much for his letter. I kiss you warmly. Greetings from us all.

The Bolsheviks did "do something," as it turned out. On December 11, 1917, after the October uprising, she wrote:

DEAR ALISA IVANOVNA!

Forgive me for not writing sooner. I'm fine, but things are a bit dull as usual. School isn't going too well. They shut off the electricity two days a week, and that means we only go to school four days. Is Ivan Ivanovich getting his newspapers? I subscribed to three of them for him. I wanted to buy him some more cigarettes, but there was such a long line I just couldn't. You have to get up before daybreak to get into the line, and even then they only give you a few. I'm having a great fight with the school. They were collecting money for the civil servants, and everybody was giving two or three rubles. When they got to me, I said, "I won't." They asked me whether I'd left my money at home. I said I just didn't want to give any. What a fuss they made. Now they all say I'm a Bolshevik, not angrily, but only teasing. I'd like to know now what party Alyosha belongs to. He's probably a Bolshevik. . . .

I've been studying music again for two months now. It's going all right, but I'm not making any promises about the future. Good-bye for now, I still have to study my wretched Bible.

The year 1918 began. Two letters to Alisa Radchenko, one in January and one in February, are full of the running of the house and a new interest: politics.

GREETINGS, DEAR ALISA IVANOVNA!

Forgive me for not writing for so long, but I got very lazy during the holidays. It's always that way. The more time you have, the lazier you are. I wish you a Happy New Year. Things are very much changed here at home. Mama's not living with us any more because we children are grown up and want to do and think as we please and not dance to our parents' tune. We're real anarchists, and that upsets her. But these are only secondary reasons, the main thing being that she can't have a life of her own here any more, and she's still young and vigorous. So I'm the one who's running the household. I've grown up a lot this past year and am quite adult now, and I'm glad.

Our schoolwork is hardly going at all. We've spent the whole week at the All-Russian Congress of Workers', Soldiers' and Peasants' Deputies. It's pretty interesting, especially when Trotsky or Lenin is speaking, but the others are very dull and don't say anything. Tomorrow, January 17, is the last day and we'll just have to go.

How are all of you? I'd especially like to know how that imp Alyoshka is. Have you any news of the Krasins?[5] They've gotten snooty for some reason and haven't answered our letters. My trouble is that I've gotten very rude and irritable, but I hope I'll get over it.

Fedya has left military school and enrolled in the mathematics

department of the Academy. I played the part of Mama and went
to fix it for him and finally it all worked out. He's working and
going to school at the same time. I'm even getting ashamed at
the way everyone else is working, while I am just lazy and spend
more money than any of them. In spite of it, they all love me.

Here is my mother's last letter from Petrograd. It was written in February, 1918.

Greetings, my dears. I'm glad you finally got the cigarettes I
sent you. Incidentally, you'll need them more now than you did
before. But why haven't you let me know whether you're getting
the newspapers I sent you or not? I was afraid of ordering them
this month for fear they don't reach you.

I'm tired of coping here at home, but it seems as if Mama will
soon be back to take over again. She's lonely without her noisy
brood. Of course we're terribly glad. My father was in bed for
three weeks. First he had a sore throat. As soon as he got better
he hurt his leg badly getting onto a streetcar. He is beginning
to get around a little now. During his illness I was housekeeper,
nurse and student all rolled into one, and had to skip three or
four days of school.

There's real hunger in Petrograd. They hand out only an
eighth of a pound of bread every day, and one day they gave us
none at all. I've even cursed the Bolsheviks. But they promise to
increase the ration on February 18. We'll see if they do or not!

I've lost twenty pounds and had to alter all my skirts and
underclothes. They were all falling off me. I've lost so much
people are even suspecting me of being in love.

Pavlusha was here for ten days and is off again. He has enlisted in the new, socialist army, though people say he's awfully
sick of being at the front. Mama scolded him for joining, but
we're all proud of him. My father wants to enlist, too, but he's
only joking, of course. How is Alyoshka? Tell him to write me
a letter. I'm sure he knows how by now.

I kiss you warmly.

Always,

NADYA

My mother was married shortly after this. She and her husband went to Moscow. She went to work under L. A. Fotiyeva[6] in Lenin's Secretariat. She and my father later left for the southern front.

Her carefree, happy childhood was over. A new life had begun, not for her alone but for the whole of Russia. She still saw something of the Radchenkos. This is her last letter to Ivan Radchenko, written six years later.

DEAR IVAN IVANOVICH!

I have an important request. If you have no objection, I earnestly ask you to give me a recommendation to enable me to go from candidate membership to full membership in the Communist Party. I wanted to ask you in person, but I had to be at the Council of People's Commissars at nine o'clock sharp and wouldn't have been able to get there on time. The recommendation should be very simple and written on a separate sheet of paper. I shall come and fetch it from you somehow, but at the moment I just can't. Forgive me for bothering you, and I thank you very much in advance.

Greetings to Alisa Ivanovna and to Alyoshka.

NADYA ALLILUYEVA

August 9, 1924

These letters have a glow of innocence and naïveté. What a child she was still! What a destiny it was that suddenly landed on her shoulders! Revolution, civil war, all the accompanying devastation—any part of this would have been enough for anybody. But this child also labored under the crushing burden of her love for a man twenty-two years older than she, a hardened revolutionary just back from exile, a man whom even his comrades found it difficult to get along with. She cast her lot with him like a tiny sailboat drawn to a giant, ocean-going steamer. This is the way I see them, plowing the turbulent ocean side by side. How long could the sailboat

keep up with the ocean liner? Could it weather the heavy
seas and not be capsized by waves that are nothing to the liner?

Even when she was still a schoolgirl and newly in love she
tried with all her might to keep up with the giant steamer.
She tried so hard that she didn't realize how much she herself
was growing, or that she was becoming a serious, wise and
mature human being in her own right—so that perhaps, by
the end, she had more understanding of things than he did
himself. Hers was a different perspective: she had only begun
to grow when the Revolution broke out, whereas he was already a man of nearly forty, an age of hardheaded skepticism
and cold calculation and all the other qualities important in a
politician.

For some reason, now that I am thirty-seven I see how different the two of them were. My mother was borne along on a
mood of romantic exaltation and youthful enthusiasm for
the Revolution that sooner or later would have had to be sup-
planted by a more mature and sober outlook. Then she would
see things somewhat differently. But let's not skip too far
ahead.

I shall go back, instead, to my early childhood because that's
when I remember her. But as you read what happened later
on, I beg you, my friend, to keep these early letters of hers constantly in mind. In her heart she never changed. She was always exactly as she was when she wrote them. Think of this
woman—so honest, innocent, conscientious and somewhat
naïve—and the world she had to live in during her twenties,
and you'll see how alien all of it was to her, and how hard.
Short as her life was, it was such that everyone who used to
come to our house has fond memories of her still. The life she
created shines in my memory to this day as the world of my
joyous childhood.

→» *9*

With her children my mother was firm and aloof. It wasn't unkindness or lack of love, but the fact that she expected a great deal of both herself and us. I always think of my mother as extremely beautiful, and I don't suppose I'm the only one who thought so. I can't remember her face, but I have the impression that she was beautiful, graceful, light of step, and that she always smelled of some nice perfume. This is how her personality and the atmosphere around her felt to me, the sort of impression a child picks up unconsciously.

She seldom kissed me or stroked my hair. My father, on the other hand, was always carrying me in his arms, giving me loud, moist kisses and calling me pet names like "little sparrow" and "little fly." Once I ruined a new tablecloth with a pair of scissors. My mother spanked me across the hands until it hurt. I cried so loud that my father came and took me by the hand. He kissed me and comforted me and quieted me down. He couldn't stand the sound of a child crying or screaming, and there were times when he saved me from cupping and mustard plasters. My mother, on the other hand, never gave in to me and scolded him for spoiling me.

This is the only letter I have from my mother to me. It was written in 1930 or '31.

HELLO, SVETLANOCHKA!

I had a letter from Vasya saying that my little girl is carrying on and being terribly naughty. I hate getting letters like that about my little girl. I thought it was a big, sensible girl I was leaving behind, and now it turns out she's only a little girl after all and doesn't know how to behave like a grownup. Svetlanochka, please talk to Natalia Konstantinovna and fix everything so I don't get any more letters like that. After you've talked to her, get Vasya or Natalia Konstantinovna to help you write me what you've decided. When Mama went away, her little girl made a great many promises, but now it turns out she isn't keeping them.

Please write and let me know whether you've decided to be good or not.

You decide. You're a big girl and are able to think for yourself. Are you reading anything in Russian? I'm waiting to hear from you.

YOUR MAMA

That was all. Not a single tender word. Yet I was a quiet, obedient child, and the misdeeds of her "big girl," who couldn't have been more than four and a half or five, must have been fairly minor. She expected a good deal of me.

My father's letters were very different. I have two letters that I think I must have gotten from him about that same time, between 1930 and 1932, because they are printed in big block letters. His letters always end: "I kiss you." My father liked to kiss me until I was grown up. And until I was about sixteen, he used to call me "Setanka." (That was what I called myself when I was little.) He also called me "Housekeeper," because he wanted me to be his housekeeper and take an active part in running the household, like my mother. Whenever I asked him for anything, he liked to answer: "Why are you only asking? Give an order, and I'll see to it right away." That's how we started the game of "orders," which we played until I was about sixteen. He thought up another game, too. He invented a perfect little girl named Lyolka as an example for me to follow. Lyolka always did just what she was supposed to, and of course I hated her for it. My father used to say he had seen Lyolka "just yesterday" and she had said such and such. Now I'll quote the letters he wrote in those years.

TO MY HOUSEKEEPER, SETANKA:
You don't write to your little papa. I think you've forgotten him. How is your health? You're not sick, are you? What are you up to? Have you seen Lyolka? How are your dolls? I thought I'd be getting an order from you soon, but no. Too bad. You're hurting your little papa's feelings. Never mind. I kiss you. I am waiting to hear from you.

LITTLE PAPA

It was all written, with great effort, in huge block letters. Here is another:

HELLO SETANKA!
Thank you for your presents. Thank you for your order, too. I see you haven't forgotten papa after all. When Vasya and his tutor go off to Moscow, stay and wait for me in Sochi. All right? I kiss you.

YOUR PAPA

Letters like this went back and forth between Sochi and Zubalovo, when my parents left us at the *dacha* and went off to Sochi in the summer, or we'd go to Sochi and they'd stay behind at the *dacha*. I've given you my father's letters right after the letter from my mother to show you the contrast in their attitudes toward their children. My father was demanding and strict with Vasily, but lenient toward me. He spoiled me and loved playing games with me. I was his rest and relaxation. My mother was more lenient with Vasily, since he already had enough discipline from my father, but was strict with me to offset my father's affection. Yet she was the one I loved more.

I remember asking my nurse one day, "Why is it I love Grandpa better than Grandma, yet I love Mama better than Papa?" My nurse was horrified. "And what about Papa and Grandma? You've got to love all of them the same. I won't hear of such a thing!" She spent a long time scolding me. She believed in loving everybody equally. That was the rule she lived by. As a good servant she also refused to have favorites among her employers, and she discouraged the children from having any favorites, either. She treated everyone exactly the same, and I was never able to detect where her own sympathies lay.

My mother spent very little time with us. She was always off somewhere. She had a great deal of work and studying to do, jobs for the Party and all sorts of other things. She saw to it that our time was filled up, too. We had our lessons. We went on outings with our tutor or nurse. We made herbariums, tended rabbits, anything to keep us from being idle! In one of her letters as a schoolgirl my mother had stated the rule that "The more time you have, the lazier you are," and it was a rule she always observed when it came to her children. Even as a tiny child I had German, Russian and arithmetic with a tutor, and drawing and modeling with my nurse.

In addition, my mother had me enrolled in a music class

for children of preschool age. There were about twenty children in the class, and it used to meet at the apartment of some people called Lomov on Spaso-Peskovsky Street off the Arbat.[1] For two years my nurse used to take me to the class on Spaso-Peskovsky Street. I enjoyed the classes very much and still remember them. We had a children's chorus and even our own soloists. We played games to improve the ear and sense of rhythm. When we were more advanced, we were taught to read and write music as well. I was good at it and my mother was very pleased. I'm sorry I can't remember the name of the nice lady who gave me my early training in music, but my nurse is dead now and I can't ask her about our teacher or about the Lomovs, at whose apartment the classes were held. The Lomovs had some good books for children. It was from them that I got *Max and Moritz*,[2] which my nurse used to read aloud. My nurse knew all the poems by heart and used to recite them to me for years afterward.

No matter how rushed she might be, my mother kept on studying music with Alexandra Pukhlyakov, a familiar figure to everyone in the Kremlin. My mother studied French, too, though I don't know who her teacher was or how far she managed to get. But the point is that she wanted to keep on learning and improving herself. She was surrounded by fine men and women of some education, and she wanted to come up to their level.

She was young and her whole life was still ahead of her. She was only thirty in 1931. She was in the Industrial Academy, studying synthetic fibers, a new branch of chemistry at the time. My mother would have made a fine specialist. Her notebooks are still in existence. They are neat and clean— they must have been model notebooks. She made excellent sketches and kept a drawing board in her room at home. She had two close friends at the Academy, A. A. Andreyev's[3] wife,

Dora Khazan, and Maria Kaganovich. The secretary of the Party Committee at the Academy was a young man named Nikita Khrushchev, who had come there straight from the Donbas. He became a full-time Party worker after he graduated from the Academy. My mother's two friends went to work in the textile industry. She longed to work on her own and hated being "first lady of the kingdom."

Once in a great while she'd spend a whole day at Zubalovo with us, probably when the governess had her day off. She'd sew and tidy things up and discuss things with the nurse and go over our exercise books. She had no time for baby talk with us children. On the other hand, when our playground was being built at Zubalovo, she thought up ways of making it more interesting. I think it was she who thought up our tree house after the one in *Robinson Crusoe*. She liked taking pictures and was very good at it. She took all the Sochi photographs and the pictures of us at Zubalovo when we were small. She would snap the children or groups of people, the trees and grass and the house itself. It's thanks to her that we have snapshots of the house at Zubalovo, the *dacha* we used to stay in at Sochi during my mother's lifetime, and the first house Merzhanov built my father in Sochi—Dacha Nine as it was called. Later my father was seized by a passion for rebuilding and did all the houses over to the point where they were no longer recognizable. I'm glad my mother took pictures of them for us to look at and remember them by.

She was the youngest person in the house except for the children. The nurse and governess were both over forty, and the cook and housekeeper over fifty. Yet all of them loved the beautiful, young, tactful lady of the house and respected her authority. She was only seven years older than my oldest brother, Yakov. She was tender and affectionate with him and took his sorrows to heart. She saw him through the death of a baby daughter and was a comfort to him throughout his unhappy first marriage. She suffered for him and tried to make him feel at home. It was difficult, however, since my father didn't approve when Yakov first came to Moscow from Georgia at the insistence of Uncle Alexander Svanidze. He disapproved of Yakov's first marriage, of how he was doing in his studies and of his character. In his eyes, Yakov could do nothing right.

My mother was terribly upset when Yakov tried to commit suicide in 1928, or it may have been 1929. In despair over the attitude of my father, who wouldn't have anything to do with him, Yakov went to the kitchen of our Kremlin apartment and shot himself. Luckily he was only wounded. My father used to make fun of him and sneer, "Ha! He couldn't even shoot straight!" My mother was horrified. The shot made a deep impression on her; her own death later on may have been an echo of it. Yakov loved me and my mother's parents. He loved and respected my mother very much. My Alliluyev grandparents looked after him as best they could. After his attempt at suicide, he went to Leningrad and lived in Grandfather's apartment.

I have a lot of pictures taken at our house. One look and it all comes back to me. The people grow and come to life under my very eyes. The black and white turns to color, the men and women move. I hear them talking to each other. They're like stills from a movie. One look and the reel starts running, which gives me the feeling that I've seen it all somewhere before.

I have pictures of picnics in the woods, which everyone enjoyed. My father is there, and so is my mother, laughing and gay. The pictures are full of smiling faces. My father, who was fifty in 1929, looks much younger than his age. My mother looks young, radiant and gracious, with a smile that shows her white teeth. The women are all very modestly dressed, but what charming faces they have.

There's my mother on the balcony at Zubalovo, sitting with

her sister Anna. There's another of her with Zina Ordzhonikidze.

There's my mother in the garden at Sochi. The Orakhelash-
vilis* are sitting on deck chairs, and Uncle Abel Yenukidze
is whittling a bamboo cane.

There's my mother on the beach at Mukholatka, in the
Crimea, where my parents used to go, with several little heads
bobbing out of the water in white panama hats—my brother
Vasily and his friends Artyom Sergeyev and Zhenya Kursky.

There's my mother on the terrace at Mukholatka, standing
beside the white marble lions. She's wearing a long, straight
dress of the kind people wore in those days. It has short sleeves
and a square neck. Her hair is combed smooth off her tanned
face and is gathered back in a bun.

There's my mother at Zubalovo, standing on the path leading through the woods to the gate. We've had high-ranking
visitors from Turkey. Apparently my father has just been
receiving them. Voroshilov, Molotov and Litvinov[4] are there.
They're all out for a walk. I'm there, too, to distract them.
My mother is wearing a shawl. She's watching nervously, to
be sure I don't do anything naughty.

There's my mother sitting by a table at Zubalovo, wearing a
shawl again. After she died my father had this picture en-
larged. The enlargements were hung in all the rooms of our
new apartment in the Kremlin. She looks so happy and radiant that looking at this picture you'd never guess what was to
happen to her later on. That's why so many people didn't
understand and couldn't believe it.

The pictures are sadder and sadder as you go on. The posed
ones taken in Moscow by N. A. Svishchov-Paola are full of
sorrow and show a woman grown weary of the world and all

* M. Orakhelashvili, Chairman of the Georgian Council of People's Commissars, arrested in 1937.

its vanities. Pride, reserve and melancholy are written on her face. You'd be afraid to go up to this woman for fear she wouldn't speak a word. The eyes have such sorrow in them that even today I can't bear to have this photograph in my room and see it all the time—such sorrow you'd think anyone could tell at a glance that this is a person who is doomed, who is dying and has to have help. Looking at it I wonder why no one tried to help her. Why couldn't anybody see how it was all going to end?

My mother had a great deal of reticence and pride. She hated to admit there was anything wrong or to discuss her private affairs. Her mother and her sister Anna were sometimes hurt by this quality of hers, since they themselves could scarcely have been more open and frank. They wore their hearts on their sleeves.

Now that I'm thirty-seven—my mother was thirty-one when she died—I understand her better than I used to. Even the little touches and details that slip out in other people's stories about her tell me a good deal.

Recently my mother's sister Anna told me that my mother used to think more and more often in her last years about leaving my father. Aunt Anna always says my mother was a "long-suffering martyr" with my father, that he was callous and harsh and inconsiderate of her feelings, and that this upset her terribly because she loved him very much. After a quarrel between them in 1926, when I was six months old, my mother took me and my brother and nurse and went up to Grandfather's in Leningrad intending to stay. She was planning to go to work and gradually build a life of her own. The quarrel was caused by some rudeness of my father's, something small in itself, but cumulative and of long standing. But my mother's anger passed. My nurse told me that my father telephoned from Moscow, wanting to come and make up and take us all home. But my mother, not without a certain malicious humor, replied, "I'll come back myself. It'll cost the state too much for you to come here." So we all went home.

Aunt Anna adds that during those last few weeks when my mother was finishing at the Academy, she meant to go to live with the Redenses in Kharkov, where he was in the Cheka, and find a job in her field there. Again and again my aunt has said that my mother was turning over in her mind the possibility of getting free of the high position that was nothing but a burden to her. Aunt Anna's story has the ring of truth. My mother never had her eye on "the main chance." The things her position gave her meant absolutely nothing to her. "Sensible," calculating women couldn't understand this at all (later on, my mother-in-law, Zinaida Zhdanov, the mother of my second husband, used to say she was "mentally unbalanced"). As they saw it, "what reason did she have," after all, to suffer and be unhappy? There was nothing any of them wouldn't have put up with to hang onto a place "at the top."

My mother, on the other hand, refused to go to the Academy in a car or even let on to the other students who she was. Many of them didn't know for a long time whom Nadya Alliluyeva was married to. Life was altogether simpler then. My father used to go out on foot like other people, though as a matter of fact he preferred going by car even then. My mother thought that even this set them apart from other people too much. She genuinely believed in the rules of Party morality which required members of the Party to live modestly. She did her best to adhere to these standards because they suited her, her parents and the other members of her family and because that was how she'd been raised.

I can give you a good example. After Lenin died, or possibly even before, the Central Committee made a ruling that members of the Party were not to keep the fees they were paid for books and articles but must donate them to the Party. My mother didn't agree. She thought it more honest to keep what you've actually earned than to give it up and spend unlimited funds belonging to the state on the upkeep of your household, on cars, *dachas,* servants and so forth. The system whereby the state paid for the households of high-ranking members of the government was only just getting under way. Thank heaven my mother didn't live to see the day when leaders of the Party, while refusing fees for their work, proceeded to maintain themselves and all their kith and kin at the expense of the state.

I believe that my mother had her own way of looking at things and stuck by it to the very end. It was not in her nature to compromise. She was part of the younger generation of the Revolution. She was one of the enthusiasts of the early Five-Year Plans, one of the dedicated builders of a new life. These were men and women of a new type. They had faith, a holy faith, in the new ideals of man set free by the Revolution from petty-bourgeois narrow-mindedness and all man's previous vices. My mother believed in this with the full fervor of revolutionary idealism, and there were people all around her whose conduct seemed to bear out her faith. It was my father who had once seemed to her the highest embodiment of the revolutionary New Man. She was a young schoolgirl and he was the friend of her parents and the uncompromising revolutionary just back from Siberia. He was to remain that to her for a long time, but not always.

Because my mother was intelligent and endlessly honest, I believe her sensitivity and intuition made her realize finally that my father was not the New Man she had thought when she was young, and she suffered the most terrible, devastating disillusionment.

My nurse told me that before she died my mother was unusually irritable and sad. One day an old friend from her school in Leningrad came to see her. They sat and talked awhile in my nursery, which also served us as the room where my mother saw visitors. My nurse heard my mother say again and again that "everything bored her," that she was "sick of everything" and "nothing made her happy." The friend asked, "What about the children?" "Everything, even the children," was my mother's reply. My nurse saw that it was so, that my mother really was tired of being alive. But it never occurred to her or to anybody else that she was capable of taking her own life within a matter of days.

As luck would have it, none of her family was in Moscow in the autumn of 1932. Pavel and the Svanidzes were in Berlin. Stanislav and Anna Redens were in Kharkov, and Grandfather Alliluyev was in Sochi. My mother was soon to graduate from the Academy and was terribly overtired.

Because of her poor nerves she wasn't supposed to touch alcohol. It had a bad effect on her. She didn't like it and was frightened, therefore, when other people had anything to drink. My father told me later that once she came home very sick after a party at the Academy at which she had had something to drink. She got cramps in her arms. My father put her to bed and comforted her. "So you love me a little after all," she said to him. He told me about this after the war. He kept coming back to the subject of my mother more and more in his later years and was always trying to find those "guilty" of her death.

The last time I saw her was on the eve of her death, or at least no more than a day or two before. She called me to her room and had me sit on her favorite *takhta,* or Georgian sofa —no one who's ever lived in the Caucasus can bear to give up the *takhta*—and spent a long time talking to me about what I ought to be like and how I ought to behave. "Don't touch alcohol!" she said. "Never drink wine!" These were echoes of her constant quarrel with my father, who in the fashion of the Caucasus was forever giving his children wine. The way she saw it, this was bound to end badly. Very likely she was right. At all events my brother Vasily finally died an alcoholic. I spent a long time sitting on her *takhta* that day. I saw my mother so rarely that I remember our last meeting very well.

"So you love me a little after all," she had said to my father, whom she had gone on loving in spite of everything. She was the sort of woman who could love only once, and she loved him with all her heart. Her mind might be against it, but once she gave her heart away, she had given it for good. My mother was a good family woman besides. Husband, home and children meant a great deal to her. So did her sense of duty. No matter how often it may have crossed her mind, therefore, I don't believe she could ever have left my father. She was too strict with herself to become the kind of woman who flits from one man to another.

People said she was too serious and strict for her age. She looked older than she was only because she was matter-of-fact and self-possessed and never let herself go. My nurse said that visits by Grandmother and Aunt Anna upset her because these two open, kindhearted women expected her to be frank. It came naturally to them to cry and complain, and she couldn't stand it.

Her self-control, her tremendous inner tension and discipline, her pent-up irritation and discontent built up more and more pressure within until finally she was like a tightly coiled spring. And when the spring uncoiled at last, it did so with ferocious force.

What caused the spring to give, the immediate occasion, was trivial in itself, so trivial one would have said it happened for no reason at all. It was a minor falling out at a banquet in honor of the fifteenth anniversary of the October Revolution. My father merely said to her, "Hey, you. Have a drink!" My mother screamed, "Don't you dare 'hey' me!" And in front of everyone she got up and ran from the table.

My nurse started telling me how it happened shortly before she died, when she already felt that she didn't have much longer to live. She didn't want to take it with her. She wanted to purge her soul of the memory as if it were her last confession. She and I sat in a little wooded place not far from where I am sitting and writing now, and she told me.

Our housekeeper, Carolina Till, always woke my mother in the morning. My mother slept in a room by herself, and my father slept either in his office or in a little room with a telephone next to the dining room. That's where he was sleeping that night, after getting home late from the banquet. My mother had come in earlier and gone to her own room.

The servants' rooms were far away, down a hallway and past the children's rooms. My father's room was to the left of the dining room. My mother's was off to the right of the dining room and down another little hall. Her windows opened onto the Alexandrovsky Garden and the Troitsky Gates. If you stand at the box office of the new Congress Hall and look to the right, across the Alexandrovsky Garden, you can see the Poteshny Palace, which is built in the old Russian style. It has a pointed roof and the windows open onto the garden. Those were my mother's windows. I don't like to look at them.

Carolina Till got up early that day as usual. She got breakfast ready and went to wake up my mother. She came running to the nursery shaking with fright and motioned to my nurse, unable to say a word. They went back together. My mother was lying beside her bed in a pool of blood. She had a little Walther pistol in her hand that Pavel had brought her from Berlin. The sound of the shot hadn't been loud enough to wake the rest of the household. The body was already cold. Faint with fear, mainly fear that my father might appear at any second, the two women laid the body on the bed and did what they could to make it look better. At a loss what to do next, they went to the telephone. They called the people who had precedence in their eyes: the chief of the Kremlin guard, Abel Yenukidze, and my mother's close friend Polina Molotov.

Everyone came running. Meantime my father slept on in his little room to the left of the dining room. Molotov and Voroshilov came. They were all in a state of shock. No one could believe it.

Finally my father woke up and came into the dining room. "Josef," they said, "Nadya is no longer with us."

That is the story my nurse told me. I trust her more than anybody because, first of all, she was totally without guile, and, secondly, because she told it to me as her confession and a simple Christian woman would never lie at such a time.

Besides, Polina Molotov, also known as Zhemchuzhina, who was a close friend of my mother's, told me something that seems to confirm it. This was in 1955, about the same time as the talk I had with my nurse, and Polina Molotov had recently returned from exile in Kazakhstan, where she was between 1949 and 1953. Because of her love for my mother, Polina Molotov had always been very good to me. My father, however, didn't like her or want me to see her and so I saw her very rarely.

Polina Molotov had been at the banquet with my mother and the others. All of them witnessed the quarrel and my mother's departure, but no one gave it much importance. Polina Molotov left the banquet with my mother so she wouldn't be alone. They went out and walked around the Kremlin Palace several times until my mother calmed down.

"She quieted down and talked about the Academy and her chances of starting to work, a prospect which occupied her mind and pleased her a good deal. Your father was rough with her and she had a hard life with him. Everyone knew that. But they'd spent a good many years together. They had a family, children, a home, and everyone loved Nadya. Who could have thought she'd ever do such a thing? It wasn't a perfect marriage, of course, but then what marriage is?

"When she seemed completely calm," Polina Molotov went on, "we went our separate ways for the night. I was perfectly sure everything was all right, that it had all subsided. And then in the morning they called to tell us the terrible news."

⇶ 10

I remember how we children were suddenly sent out at an unusual hour that morning to play. I remember how Natalia Konstantinovna kept wiping her eyes with a handkerchief at breakfast. For some reason we spent a long time out playing. Suddenly we were taken to the *dacha* at Sokolovka. This was a dark, dismal place where we had started going that fall instead of our beloved Zubalovo. It was always fearfully gloomy at Sokolovka. The big downstairs room got very little light, and there were dark places and corners everywhere. The rooms were cold, uncomfortable and strange. Later that day Voroshilov came. He took us walking and tried to play with us, but he was weeping. I don't remember how they told me my mother was dead or how I took it. I've forgotten, probably because the idea of death didn't have any meaning for me then.

111

I began to realize something had happened only when they took me to the building where GUM is now, but which was then an official building of some kind. The open coffin with the body was standing in a big room and a leavetaking ceremony was being held. I was terribly frightened when Zina Ordzhonikidze took me by the hand and led me right up to my mother's face and told me to "say good-bye." Probably I sensed the presence of death for I gave a loud cry and drew back. Someone quickly carried me into another room. Uncle Abel Yenukidze took me on his knees. He played with me and gave me fruit to eat. Once again I forgot about death. I wasn't taken to the funeral. Only Vasily went.

Later, when I was grown up, I was told that my father had been terribly shaken. He was shaken because he couldn't understand why it had happened. What did it mean? Why had such a terrible stab in the back been dealt to him, of all people? He was too intelligent not to know that people always commit suicide in order to punish someone. He saw that, but he couldn't understand why. What was he being punished for?

He asked those around him whether it was true he'd been inconsiderate. Hadn't he loved and respected her as a wife and human being? Was it really so important if he hadn't always been able to go to the theater with her? Did it make that much difference?

The first few days he was in a state of shock. He said he didn't want to go on living either. I was told this by Uncle Pavel's widow, who with Aunt Anna stayed with us day and night. My father was in such a state that they were afraid to leave him alone. He had sporadic fits of rage. The reason is that my mother had left him a letter.

Apparently she wrote it the night she died. Needless to say, I've never seen it. Very likely it was destroyed right away, but people who actually saw it have told me of its existence. It was a terrible letter, full of reproaches and accusations. It wasn't purely personal; it was partly political as well. After reading it, it would have been possible for my father to think that my mother had been on his side only outwardly, but that in her heart she had been on the side of those who were in political opposition to him.

He was shocked and incensed. At the civil leavetaking ceremony he went up to the coffin for a moment. Suddenly he pushed it away from him, turned on his heel and left. He didn't even go to the funeral.

My mother was buried by her relatives and friends. Uncle Abel Yenukidze, her godfather, was the one who walked first behind the coffin. It was a long time before my father regained his equilibrium. He never went to visit her grave at Novo-Devichy. Not even once. He couldn't. He thought my mother had left him as his personal enemy.

It was only in his last years, not long before he died, that he suddenly started talking to me about it, nearly driving me out of my mind. I saw that he was desperately looking for the reason—looking, and not finding it. Suddenly he would start denouncing the "vile book" which my mother had read not long before she died. It was *The Green Hat* by Michael Arlen, which was very much in vogue at that time. He thought it had had an important effect on her. Then he started blaming Polina Molotov, Aunt Anna and Pavel, who had brought her a pistol so tiny it looked like a toy. He was trying to discover "who was guilty" and "who put her up to it." Maybe he thought that if he could figure that out, he would have uncovered an important enemy of his own.

But if he failed to understand her at the time, then later, after twenty years, he no longer understood her at all and must have forgotten what she was like. One good thing, though, is that twenty years later he started speaking about

her more gently. He even seemed to pity her and no longer
blamed her for what she had done.

People shot themselves fairly often in those days. Trotsky-
ism had been defeated. Collectivization of the farms had just
gotten under way. The Party was torn by opposition and fac-
tional strife. One leading Party member after another did
away with himself. Mayakovsky had shot himself only a short
time before. People couldn't make sense of this, and the
memory was still very fresh.

I think all this couldn't fail to have had its effect on my
mother, impulsive and susceptible as she was. The Alliluyevs
were all sensitive and high-strung, quivering with sensibility.
They had the temperament of which artists, not politicians,
are made. As Pushkin put it: "You don't hitch a horse and a
quivering doe to the same cart."

The point is, my mother's whole life was lived by the laws
of feeling. Hers was a poet's logic. Mayakovsky had said a
short time before he died, "I won't hurl myself down a stair
well, I won't sip poison, I cannot cock the rifle to my temple."
So saying, he did precisely that.

No one plans things like this ahead of time.

My mother had great intelligence. My father respected her.
He believed in her implicitly and up to the moment of her
death considered her his trusted and closest friend. Yet with
all her discipline and restraint, my mother was a woman of
strong feelings.

People were a lot more honest and emotional in those days.
If they didn't like life the way it was, they shot themselves.
Who does that kind of thing now? Who cares that much about
life and differences of opinion, about his own convictions or
those of his opponents, or about whether one course of action
is better than another?

The spirit of skepticism has taken over—skepticism and in-difference to all that is most precious and vital. "Who cares? I'll get by" is the spirit of the present day.

People were different then. My mother was a child of her time. If she hadn't been so young, it probably would have passed. But the time of cool calculation hadn't come on her yet at the age of thirty-one.

I often wonder what sort of life she'd have had if she'd lived. It couldn't have been good. Sooner or later she'd have sided with the opposition to my father. She couldn't have looked on in silence as all the best of her good old friends perished—Bukharin, Yenukidze, Redens and both the Svan-idzes. She could never have survived it.

Maybe fate gave her the gift of death to spare her the still greater disasters that lay in store. "Quivering doe" that she was, she could never have prevented these disasters, much less have put an end to them once they were under way.

→≫ *11*

The day before yesterday, my friend, I wrote you the thing that was hardest of all. Thinking about it and, even worse, writing about it are always a terrible ordeal. The older I get, the more painful it is for me to think about it.

That same day before yesterday, luckily for me, some good friends of mine dragged me off to the Istra Reservoir. I know some people who live near there. In winter we all go skiing together here, near Zhukovka. My friends had no idea how grateful I was to them for taking me away.

We turned off past Istra, onto the Buzharovo road. I was surrounded on all sides by calm, eternal Nature, vast as the sky and heedless of everything. What miraculous places! What gentle, still, incomparable beauty!

The ocean is splendid, of course. The south is luxuriant,

and mountains are more impressive. But the gray huts that
have been standing here so many years, these fields and meadows, the woods on the horizon and the sky that's now blue
and now gray above—what is the magic of all this? And this
sweet clover that's growing along the road, all yellow and white.
You crush the blossoms in your hand and they smell of honey.
Can the roses of the south compare with this fragrance?
There's the Istra itself, its water sluggish and dark green, its
winding banks overgrown with willows. You can't swim there.
You just look and look and feel a tightening of the throat
from so much quiet beauty, and it would be good to cry, as
if a friend you haven't seen in a long time suddenly appears
and you put your head on his shoulder and weep for joy.

The reservoir is nature itself, majestic and powerful. The
surface shimmers and dances in the sun, and the shore is
overgrown with trees, with birches and pines. There's a sandy
shore and tiny rippling waves. And there are tents, cars, young
faces, sun-tanned bodies, bright bathing suits, and young people everywhere. Some are on bicycles. Others are on foot with
knapsacks on their backs. Still others are in cars with boats
strapped onto the roof. All over the world people want the
same thing—a good and healthy life.

When we got to Alekhnovo we drove to the very last house.
Beyond it there's a cabbage field. The village houses are nice
and clean. And the fields are surprisingly well tended. Everything is better kept up than where I live, in Krasnogorsk District on the outskirts of Moscow. It seems an agronomist named
Schmidt has been chairman of the collective farm in Alekhnovo for several years now. He came here from Moscow
when they were drafting specialists and sending them to the
countryside. Many of them weren't any good, but some of
them knew their business. Schmidt—people think he's a Jew,
but he's really a Russian of German extraction—did a lot for

the collective farm, and now there are gardens and vegetables and grain growing everywhere. The people are pretty well off. Not much is needed, really, but a little keenness and capacity to organize, a bit of initiative and education.

It was light long after we got there that evening. The village is in the fields and the reservoir is nearby. Above its even, level surface was a wide expanse of open sky. Light poured from it for hours, first the red of sunset, then violet, then at last the deep blue of twilight. It was so still, the air thick with the sweet, heady smell of grass. A round silver moon came sailing out from behind the woods. The air grew more and more fragrant. It was damp underfoot, and the air became a deeper and deeper violet. The stars started lighting up one after the other overhead so that at last they seemed to close in on you and there were so many it was impossible to think of anything else. I lay down on a camp bed in the farmyard under the open sky. The stars twinkled and I wanted to weep from joy at being alive and breathing those sweet-smelling grasses and seeing those stars above me.

We spent all the next day walking and swimming in the reservoir and admiring it from a steep place. A field of wheat shone all gold behind us and giant, fluffy white clouds were unfurling over the water.

Then a storm cloud appeared from nowhere. It billowed and filled up and grew black under our very eyes, and the whole sky suddenly clouded over. Only the wheat field was still yellow and went on glowing as before. There was a peal of thunder, and rain came pouring down and suddenly turned to hail. Yet even as it was happening, it rolled far, far into the distance over the glassy water and part of the sky above us became blue again.

Slender shafts of gold broke from behind the rain cloud. They pierced the clouds that remained and quickly scattered them. The sun came out again and started shining and dried up the raindrops all around us. The freshly washed earth was so lovely I wanted to gasp for joy. And the rest of the day I was choked up with tears.

It all passed as though it had never been, neither clouds nor rain. An hour later it was hot again, and everything was parched all around, and tourists were baking on the sand again, and the little boats came floating across the water from every side.

That evening we went home, rested and refreshed after only one day. I looked around me with joy and sorrow and wondered where I had ever gotten such love of Russia.

We are barbarians of a type you'll find nowhere else on earth. The Georgians, the Uzbeks and the Ukrainians preserve every wall, every glazed potsherd of antiquity as if it were a treasure and a jewel. But as Pushkin said, "We are lazy and lacking in curiosity." There are the loveliest church and bell tower on a hill not far from Alekhnovo. By some miracle they survived the bombardments of the last war. Old lindens, like sentries, surround them. Yet the church, a simple cube with a cupola on top, is falling down and has an elder bush growing out of the roof. Potatoes and hay are now stored inside.

No country on earth wastes its own heritage, its ancient treasures as we do, simply out of slothfulness. No revolution ever destroyed so much of value for the people as our Russian Revolution. Even now, when we do so much talking about our Russian traditions, it's only idle words.

In spite of her mixed blood my mother, of course, was Russian, a real Russian by temperament and upbringing. My father loved Russia deeply all his life. I know no other Georgian who had so completely sloughed off his qualities as a

Georgian and loved everything Russian the way he did. Even in Siberia my father had a real love of Russia—the nature, the people, the language. He always looked back on his years of exile as if they were nothing but hunting, fishing and walks through the taiga. This love remained with him always.

And what shall I say of myself! How well I understand the Russians who fled to France, where life wasn't so easy either, and then came home again. I also understand those who refused to go and live with relatives abroad after returning from prisons and labor camps—they just couldn't bring themselves to leave Russia. But I don't have to tell you this. No matter how cruel and harsh our country may be, no matter how often we stumble and are hurt, no matter how many undeserved wrongs we may endure, no one who loves Russia in his heart will ever betray her or give her up or run away in search of material comfort. Her beauty, tranquil and wise, shines like a soft, sorrowful light from the pale sky. It will survive everything and go on forever.

After such cruel bereavements, after so many disappointments and losses, after thirty-seven years of a foolish, pointless, hopeless, double life, I see you shining, my beloved, chaotic, all-knowing, heartless Russia. You comfort me and light the way. Nothing will ever blacken you in my eyes. If your goodness and truth hadn't lit my way, I'd have given up long ago. You are warmth and light. You make me feel that life on this beautiful green earth I love so well still holds some promise.*

---

* Four years ago, when I wrote this, it never crossed my mind that I would ever be capable of leaving Russia. At that time everybody lived in the hope that fundamental changes in the direction of real democracy might still take place.

⇥ 12

For ten years after my mother died, my father was a good father to me. It wasn't easy with the kind of life he led, but he did his best. Although our home life was shattered, from the time I was six until I was sixteen my father was the final, unquestioned authority for me in everything. Then, beginning in 1942 or 1943, the end of school and certain other events caused things to change a good deal. Our relationship changed, too. We became estranged, and later it only got worse.

Our carefree life, so full of gaiety and games and useful pastimes, fell apart the moment my mother died.

In the summer of 1933, when we went to Zubalovo, I found that the playground in the woods with its hoops and swings

121

and its Robinson Crusoe tree house had vanished so completely it might have been swept away by a broom. The only thing left was some traces of sand in the woods. Then it was all overgrown.

Our governess, Natalia Konstantinovna, whose lessons in German, drawing and reading I'll never forget as long as I live, left right away. Whether she left voluntarily or was dismissed I don't know, but the rhythm of our studies was broken. My brother's tutor, Alexander Muravyov, lasted another two years. But then Vasily got annoyed with him because he sometimes tried to make him work. So he, too, disappeared.

My father moved to a different apartment because he couldn't bear to stay in the one my mother had died in. He started building the house at Kuntsevo where he lived for the next twenty years. The rest of us kept on going to Zubalovo on Sundays, during vacations and in the summer. My father spent little time at the new apartment in the Kremlin and only came there at night, to eat. It was most uncomfortable to live in. It was on the first floor of the Senate building. Before, it had been nothing but a long, official corridor with rooms to one side. It had walls nearly five feet thick and high, vaulted ceilings.

These rooms, which had been offices, were converted into an apartment for my father because his office, the office of the Chairman of the Council of Ministers and First Secretary of the Communist Party, was in the same building one floor above, and all he had to do was go down a floor and he was home for dinner. After dinner, which generally started between six and seven in the evening and went on till eleven or twelve, he'd get into his car and go out to Kuntsevo. At two or three the next day he'd be at his office in the Central Committee. That was his routine until the war.

His time for seeing me and Vasily was during dinner at the apartment. He'd ask me about my lessons, look at the book my marks were entered in and sometimes ask me to show him my exercise books. He used to sign the book containing my marks, as parents were supposed to do, right up to the war, and he signed Vasily's until he went off to special aviation school in 1939. So we all saw each other often, practically every day.

Also, he continued taking us with him to Sochi in the summer. Grandfather, Grandmother, Uncle Pavel and his wife, the Redenses and the Svanidzes still came to see him. They'd all go to my father's at Kuntsevo for birthdays and New Year's. And we all went to Sochi on vacation together.

But inwardly things had changed catastrophically. Something had snapped inside my father. And the household had changed.

It didn't change all at once, but by 1937 or 1938, except for my nurse, there was no one left of the people my mother had found, of the people who loved and respected her, who remembered and still tried to adhere to her ways of doing things. As the years went by all of them gradually vanished. One year I came back for school in September to find that our old cook, Elizaveta, was gone. She was a strapping, severe, regal woman with a high, old-fashioned hairdo, a real Catherine the Great. They had driven her out. Later they got rid of Tanya, a big woman who used to carry the heavy kitchen trays. She was fearfully ugly, but very good-natured and cheerful.

Finally our housekeeper, Carolina Till, left too. It was 1937, and her German ancestry probably had something to do with it. So in spite of the fact that she'd been with us ten years and was practically a member of the family, she, too, was thrown out. The whole staff at Zubalovo was changed, and new people whom none of us knew appeared at my father's house in Kuntsevo as well.

But the main thing was that the whole way of running the

house was changed. My mother used to find servants whom she liked for their qualities as people, and she paid them out of her own modest funds. But now the entire household was run at state expense. At once the size of the staff, or "service personnel," as they called it to avoid the old bourgeois word "servants," increased enormously. At each of my father's houses there suddenly appeared commandants, a detail of bodyguards each with a chief of its own, two cooks to take turns during the day, and a double staff of waitresses and cleaning women, also working in two shifts. These people were all handpicked by a special section for personnel, and, of course, once they had been appointed as part of the household staff, they automatically became employees of the MGB (or GPU, as the secret police were still known).

My nurse had a hard time of it. She looked like an odd duck among all these minions. So although she had always gotten along famously with everyone around her, they decided to get rid of her too. In 1939, when people were still disappearing right and left, somebody, probably some personnel man with nothing better to do, came up with the information that my nurse's husband, whom she left during World War I, had been a clerk in the Czarist police before the Revolution. They told my father that my nurse was "untrustworthy" and that her son had undesirable friends.

My father had no time to go into these things himself. He liked having the people whose job it was go into such matters thoroughly and only bring them to his attention when they had "closed their case." When I heard there was a plot afoot to get rid of my nurse, I set up an outcry. My father couldn't stand tears. Besides, maybe he, too, wanted to express some inner protest against all this insanity. In any case, he got angry all of a sudden and commanded them to leave my nurse in peace. She was a member of the family thirty years in all, from 1926 to 1956, when she died at the age of seventy. I'll tell you about her later.

Our household staff grew by leaps and bounds. It wasn't just in our house that the new system was put into effect, but in the houses of all the members of the government, at least the ones who belonged to the Politburo. No household, however, had such an official, even quasi-military, atmosphere as ours. None was so subject to the orders of the secret police. The reason was that my father was a widower. The presence of a wife mitigated and restrained the spread of bureaucracy a little in the other households. In principle, however, all of them were the same. They were all paid for out of government funds and maintained by government employees who kept their masters under close surveillance night and day.

The system started in the early thirties and rapidly took hold. It was only with Beria's elimination that the Central Committee realized how vital it was for the secret police to be put in their place. Only then did people start living differently and breathing more freely, members of the government no less than ordinary mortals.

The waitresses we had liked so much, Klavdia and Zina, were banished from Zubalovo. There were new ones now, among them a young one with a snub nose and a gay, ringing laugh called Valechka. After three years at Zubalovo she was transferred to my father's *dacha* at Kuntsevo. She eventually worked as his housekeeper and remained there until he died.

Sergei Yefimov, who was commandant at Zubalovo while my mother was still alive, stayed on with us a little longer, but was then transferred to my father's household at Kuntsevo. Of all the "chiefs," he was the most decent and the one least out for himself. He was always good to us children and to those of our relatives who survived. He had at least some vestiges of human feeling toward us as a family. The other bodyguards had very little such feeling. I don't even want to think of their names. The one thing they wanted was to grab as much as they could for themselves. They all built themselves country houses and drove government cars and lived like ministers and even members of the Politburo, and all of them now bemoan the material benefits they've lost.

Yefimov wasn't like that. He, of course, lived well, too, but on a modest scale compared with the others. He didn't live like a minister, for example, though it must be said that a member of the Academy of Sciences might have envied his apartment and his house in the country. Toward the end of my father's lifetime Yefimov, by that time a general in the secret police, fell out of favor with him. He was removed and "eaten alive" by his colleagues, the other generals and colonels of the police who constituted a peculiar kind of "court" around my father.

I must now mention another general, Nikolai Vlasik, who was first assigned to my father by the Red Army as a body-guard in 1919 and remained with him for a very long time, finally attaining immense power behind the scenes. He was in charge of all my father's security arrangements and considered himself closer to my father than anybody else. And though he was incredibly stupid, illiterate and uncouth, he behaved like a grandee and took it on himself in my father's last years to dictate "Comrade Stalin's tastes," which he thought he knew well, to various luminaries in the arts. And they had to listen and take his advice. No Bolshoi gala performance on the eve of November 7 or state banquet in St. George's Hall of the Kremlin was allowed to take place without Vlasik's passing on the program first. His insolence knew no bounds. He would graciously pass the word to people in the arts whether this or that movie or opera or even the shapes of the skyscrapers being built in those days had found favor or not with my father.

He did a lot to spoil our lives and wouldn't be worth mentioning at all except that he was the kind of colorful personality you can't ignore. As far as the household staff was concerned, the name "Vlasik" was nearly as important as that of my father himself. My father, after all, was way up there on his pinnacle, and it was in Vlasik's power to do anything he liked. While my mother was alive he remained somewhere in the background as a member of my father's bodyguard and never set foot in the house. Later, however, he was a permanent fixture of the household at Kuntsevo. From there he ran all my father's other residences, which became more and more numerous as the years went by.

In addition to Kuntsevo and Zubalovo, where various members of the family were still living quietly, my father had two other places outside Moscow alone. They were Lipki, an ancient estate on the Dmitrov Highway with a pond, a wonderful house and an enormous park lined with tall lindens, and Semyonovskoye, a fine old estate that had a house built just before the war, large, spring-fed ponds dug by serfs in the old days, and extensive woods. Now it's a "government *dacha*." Some celebrated meetings between Party leaders and writers and artists have taken place there.[1]

At Lipki and Semyonovskoye everything was exactly as it was at Kuntsevo. The rooms were the same and had the same furniture and there were exactly the same flowers and bushes outside the house. Vlasik would give the word as to what "the boss" did or didn't like. My father seldom visited either place, sometimes not for a year at a time, but the staff always expected him at any moment and was in a perpetual ·state of readiness. And if a motorcade actually did take off from Kuntsevo in the direction of Lipki, pandemonium would break loose there and everyone from the cook to the guard at the gate, from the waitresses to the commandant, would be seized by panic. They all awaited these visitations like Judgment Day, but the one they were most frightened of was the crude martinet Vlasik, who loved shouting at them and giving them all hell.

Also worthy of interest as a specimen all too typical of those times was our new Kremlin housekeeper, Lieutenant (later Major) of the State Security Forces Alexandra Nakashidze. She appeared in 1937 or 1938 through the good offices of Beria, to whom she was related, being a cousin of his wife's. But she didn't count for much in the family. Beria's wife, for example, detested her and thought she was stupid. That didn't make the slightest difference, however, since her appointment was decided without her knowledge or, indeed, without the knowledge of either of them. So one fine day this rather good-looking young woman had the pleasure of becoming our housekeeper.

One September I got back from Sochi as usual and to my astonishment was met in the front hallway not by Carolina Till but by a rather flustered Georgian girl instead. This was to be our new housekeeper.

She didn't mean any harm, and did more damage because she wasn't very bright and because of what the job required than because she actually wanted to hurt anyone. Besides, she was a newcomer in a house where life had become very lonely. So she and I made friends and were on good terms until 1942 or 1943, when she and Vlasik did me a bad turn. At first, moreover, being only eleven or twelve, I was too young to appreciate how grotesque it was to have Beria's own personal spy in the house.

My aunts Anna and Evgenia, Pavel's widow, realized right away what it was all about and merely inquired whether she knew how to run a house and prepare Georgian food. "Why, no," Alexandra Nakashidze replied innocently. "I never did anything at home. My mother did all the housework and I never even washed my own cup." Even my aunts were a bit taken aback by that and said something to the effect that "It'll be hard for you here then." But then they shrugged, realizing that the skills she needed as an operative of the NKVD had nothing to do with cooking.

Soon after this, incidentally, my aunts were barred from our Kremlin apartment. Redens had been arrested, and since the sudden death of her husband Evgenia was suspected of having poisoned him. Yakov and my grandparents were the only ones still allowed to come there. Probably Alexandra Nakashidze had informed on my aunts to Beria and he decided that these people had been "hanging around" Stalin long enough and that it was time to isolate him from them and the breath of fresh air they brought with them. For an intriguer of Beria's talents it didn't take much to convince my father that as "relatives of persons who have been repressed"[2] they aroused doubts and apprehension.

Alexandra Nakashidze ruled the roost in our apartment until 1943. How and why my father himself threw her out I'll tell you later. One of her duties was to get as close as she could to Vasily and me. She was a giggly woman of barely thirty, who was fairly new to her work for the secret police and hadn't yet acquired the manner that went with it. In any case, Georgian women aren't cut out for that sort of thing. She was kind enough, on the whole, and it was only natural for her to make friends with us in a house where she was strange and her own duties frightened her. She was a hapless pawn, caught in a monstrous system that wouldn't let her make a single move of her own. She had no choice but to do what they demanded of her, to the extent that her poor brain and meager capacities would allow.

My school work was the responsibility of others, but she used to go to the theater with me and assumed over-all guidance, as it were, of my upbringing. Sometimes she even had a look at my exercise books. She spoke Russian poorly and wrote it even worse. She was in no position to check on my progress and she knew it. But she checked on my school friends and other acquaintances. The circle of people I knew was so narrow and circumscribed and my little world so tiny that this didn't give her any trouble.

Life wasn't easy for her in our house, and I'm sure she was grateful when she was finally told to go. To brighten her lonely, cheerless existence, she brought her father, mother, sister and two brothers up from Georgia. They were all given apartments in Moscow, and the brothers and sister were able to marry and settle down.

She set about putting our house in order—not my father's rooms, of course, since no one was allowed in there or permitted to touch anything, but my room and Vasily's. She threw out all the furniture my mother had given us, on the ground that it was too old-fashioned and that we ought to be more up to date. One year when I got back from the south I didn't recognize my own room. Where was the old, carved sideboard given me by my mother, where I kept all the presents she and Aunt Maria had brought me from Berlin? And the countless other presents from Aunt Anna? I had kept the bright clay figures Natalia Konstantinovna taught us to make on the top shelves and old albums of drawings and exercises in German and Russian on the bottom. My nurse had thought it a good idea to keep them.

But Alexandra Nakashidze, who doubtless considered herself a woman of culture—she had had two years at the Tbilisi Industrial Institute before going to work for the secret police —thought it was all a lot of nonsense. She threw out the cupboard and everything in it without stopping to realize that she was throwing out my most cherished childhood mementos.

She likewise got rid of a round table and some chairs my mother had put in my nursery. And she replaced it all by furniture which was, indeed, more modern, but cold, unfamiliar and utterly lacking in character—objects that meant nothing to me or to anybody else.

She did the same with my brother's room and took away every reminder of our comfortable old apartment where everything was my mother's creation and which my mother had adapted to our needs and convenience.

My nurse suffered all this in silence. She realized it wouldn't do any good to object and thought it was better to put up with it for the time being and get on with the business of rearing her unfortunate charge. And so she looked on indignantly, but meekly and without a murmur, as they got rid of all my cherished old things—though some of them she managed to send to her granddaughter Katya in the country, who was a little younger than I.

I kept on the dressing table the very few knickknacks left by my mother. There was a beautiful enameled box with dragons on it, some cups and a tiny glass. Bit by bit, these things all disappeared, too, though I've no idea what became of them. Everything vanished, and we came to realize that under the new system everything in the house was considered state property and anything old and dilapidated would be "inventoried" each year and carted off God knew where. Later I saw some of them in the apartment of Alexandra Nakashidze's brother and sister.

My father seemed very remote from all of us. Once in a while he gave our unofficial guardian Vlasik over-all directives on how we were to be brought up. We were to be fed, clothed and shod at state expense, not luxuriously or with frills, but solidly and well. No one was to spoil us; we were to spend as much time as possible in the fresh air at Zubalovo. We were to go south in summer to Sochi or to Mukholatka in the Crimea. These instructions were carried out faithfully, but in such a loose way that in fact we were left very much to our own devices.

It was in line with some directive of this kind that a governess named Lidia Georgiyevna appeared on the scene unexpectedly about the time I first went to school. I was unpleasantly struck by the way she looked. She was very small and hunchbacked, with dyed red hair. She and my nurse had a fight the very first day. I've no idea what started it. All I know is that I saw my nurse leave the room obviously offended and heard Lidia Georgiyevna cry out, "Remember your place, Comrade Bychkov! You've no right to talk to me like that!"

I took one look and told her calmly, "Fool. Don't you dare insult my nurse!"

She had hysterics. She laughed and sobbed at the same time, a thing I'd never seen before, and called both of us names. I was "an ill-mannered girl" and my nurse was "uncultured."

The quarrel died down, but she and I were now enemies forever. She taught me German and was supposed to "help" me with my homework. But compared with the lively, interesting lessons of Natalia Konstantinovna it was all a grinding bore. Thanks to her I learned to hate German. I came to hate music as well—the piano, the pieces and exercises I had to play, my scales and even the sight of the notes themselves—all because she rammed them down my throat without a glimmer of understanding.

She "brought me up" for five years, turning up every day to carry on a running fight with my even-tempered nurse and make my life a torment with her hysterics, her dreary lessons and her uninspired methods of teaching. I was spoiled for life by the splendid teachers my mother had found for me.

After five years I could stand it no longer and implored my

father to get rid of her. My father had no special sympathy for a hunchbacked old maid who flirted with every man in sight. This alone was enough to make him wince, and I was set free of her.

That was the end of governesses for me. My father had now made up his mind that everything else could go by the board but I simply had to learn English. So from time to time various English teachers would appear. One of them was a nice, cheerful, fat little lady with a large braid around her head by the name of Tatyana Vasilchikova. She and I became friends, and on vacations she went to Sochi with me. I enjoyed her lessons and got a good deal out of them.

Once his tutor Alexander Muravyov had gone, Vasily's school work got worse and worse. His teachers and the head of his school bombarded my father with complaints about his behavior and his lack of progress. My father ranted and raved. He scolded Vasily and blamed Vlasik, my aunts and the entire household for his bad grades, but things didn't get any better. In the end my brother switched to artillery school and then to the aviation institute at Kacha, in the Crimea. He went there in 1939, and my nurse and I were the only ones left at home.

I'll tell you a little about some of the other bizarre characters who watched over me during those years. Starting in 1937, someone—I don't know whether it was my father, Vlasik or some committee of the secret police—decided that a plainclothes man was to follow at my heels everywhere I went: to the country, the theater, to and from school every day. He was supposed to protect me, though from whom and what I never had the faintest idea.

The first was an emaciated, jaundiced-looking man, Ivan Krivenko by name. When I saw him rummaging in my schoolbag and reading my diary, which I was taking to show to my friends, I conceived a hatred for him. He was quickly replaced by a fat, self-important-looking man named Alexander Volkov, who bit by bit terrorized the whole school.* He inaugurated a system of his own there. Instead of using the same cloakroom as everybody else, I had to use a special little room next to the school office, to which I would go blushing with embarrassment and rage. During the midday break, instead of eating in the dining room with my friends, I had to have a lunch brought specially from home, in a little corner screened off from everybody else. I stood it awhile and then rebelled.

Next I had a quiet, goodhearted man by the name of Mikhail Klimov. He and I were even friends, in a way, despite the unsavory nature of his duties. He trudged faithfully behind me from 1940 to 1943, when the job was abolished altogether. I was in my first year at the university by then. I told my father I was ashamed to go there with this "tail" and begged him to take it off. Apparently my father realized how absurd the whole thing was. He was just back from the Teheran Conference of December, 1943, and was in a particularly good frame of mind. He simply said, "To hell with you, then. Get killed, if you like. It's no business of mine." And that was the end of that. I was seventeen and a half, in other words, before I was allowed to go to the theater, the movies or the university, or even walk down the street, by myself.

Mikhail Klimov and I, however, parted on friendly terms. He liked the fact that we went to the theater all the time. He loved plays, though he didn't care much for opera. But the Conservatory, for which I then had a passion, left him cold. "Where are we going today, Svetochka?" he'd ask. He'd clutch his head if I told him we were going to a concert. "Oh, those rusty saws again! What do you see in that stuff?" But duty required it of him, and he'd fall quietly asleep unless the

* Between 1933 and 1943 I attended what was called Model School No. 25 on Staro-Pimenovsky Street, off Gorky Street.

music had too much bravura or there was too much "sawing" of violins.

Sometimes he calls me up even now, as do Valechka and Sergei Yefimov. He wants to know how I am and how the children are and to tell me about his family.

He bore me no ill will and didn't do any damage. He even pitied me, in a way, because he saw how grotesque my life was. Like Alexandra Nakashidze, he was just a little man who had to do what he was told and didn't himself want to do anybody any harm. What was wrong was the whole monstrous system, the hideous mechanism. Only now that I'm grown up do I see what it was all about. At the time it was clear only to adults, people with experience and wisdom in the ways of the world. People with heads on their shoulders saw how terrible it all was at the time and didn't have to wait until the Twentieth Party Congress to see the light, as some of them are saying now.

So there it is. That's what our home, if you can call it that, was like until the outbreak of the war.

Grandfather and Grandmother still were living at Zubalovo. The rest of us visited from time to time and stayed there during the summer. We also used to visit my father's house at Kuntsevo, and we all used to go together to Sochi, where we saw the three wonderful new houses which Merzhanov had built for him there. One was at Sochi, on a site not far from Matsesta which my mother had helped to choose. Another was at Kholodnaya Rechka, just before you get to Gagra. The third was near the Myussera River, a little past Adler.

Both the Svanidzes, Uncle Pavel and the Redenses still used to come to our Kremlin apartment. But with my mother gone nothing was the same. Everything had collapsed: the sense of a home, relationships, the feeling of friendly concern each one had for all the others.

I remember vividly the last time Uncle Alexander Svanidze

came to the apartment at the Kremlin. He looked sad and depressed. He must have known all too well what was going on. People were being arrested in Georgia, where Beria got his start. He sat in my room a long time waiting for my father. He kissed me and played with me and let me sit on his lap. My father arrived. He generally brought the people who had been in the office with him all day so they could talk about work over dinner. He almost never came alone. It can hardly have been easy for Uncle Alexander to talk to him in front of the others.

It was as if my father were making a point of cutting himself off from his relatives, his family and all their concerns.

My mother's death was a dreadful, crushing blow, and it destroyed his faith in his friends and people in general. He had always considered my mother his closest and most faithful friend. He viewed her death as a betrayal and a stab in the back. He was embittered by it. Probably whenever he saw any member of her family it was a painful reminder of her. So he started avoiding them.

With typical cunning Beria played on my father's bitterness and sense of loss. Up to then he had simply been an occasional visitor to the house in Sochi when my father was on vacation there. Now that he had my father's sympathy and support, however, he quickly wormed his way up to the job of First Secretary of the Georgian Communist Party. Olga Shatunov-skaya told me that the Party people in Georgia were appalled and Ordzhonikidze stubbornly opposed it, but that my father wouldn't give an inch.

Once he was First Secretary in Georgia, it didn't take Beria long to reach Moscow, where he began his long reign in 1938. From then on he saw my father every day. His influence on my father grew and grew and never ceased until the day of my father's death.

I speak advisedly of his influence on my father and not the other way around. Beria was more treacherous, more practiced in perfidy and cunning, more insolent and single-minded than my father. In a word, he was a stronger character. My father had his weaker sides. He was capable of self-doubt. He was cruder and more direct than Beria, and not so suspicious. He was simpler and could be led up the garden path by someone with Beria's craftiness. Beria was aware of my father's weaknesses. He knew the hurt pride and the inner loneliness. He was aware that my father's spirit was, in a sense, broken. And so he poured oil on the flames and fanned them as only he knew how. He flattered my father with a shamelessness that was nothing if not Oriental. He praised him and made up to him in a way that caused old friends, accustomed to looking on my father as an equal, to wince with embarrassment.

Beria's role was a terrible one for all our family. How my mother feared and hated him! And it was her friends—Alexander Svanidze, his wife Maria, his sister Mariko who was Yenukidze's secretary, to say nothing of Yenukidze himself —who were the first to fall, the moment Beria was able to convince my father that they were hostile to him.

I have already said that in a good many things Beria and my father were guilty together. I'm not trying to shift the blame from one to the other. At some point, unfortunately, they became spiritually inseparable. The spell cast on my father by this terrifying evil genius was extremely powerful, and it never failed to work.

Olga Shatunovskaya has told me that Beria's role in the Civil War in the Caucasus was highly ambiguous. He was a born spy and *provocateur*. He worked first for the Dashnakists (the Armenian nationalists) and then for the Reds as power swung back and forth. Once the Reds caught him in the act of treason and had him arrested. He was in prison awaiting sentence when a telegram arrived from Kirov, who was chief of all operations in the Caucasus, demanding that he be shot as a traitor. Just then, however, the fighting started up again, and he was such small fry that nobody got around to dealing with him. But all the Old Bolsheviks in the Caucasus knew of the telegram's existence—and Beria himself knew of it. Isn't it perhaps here that one should seek an explanation of Kirov's murder many years later? It was right after Kirov's murder in 1934, after all, that Beria began his climb to prominence and power. It's at least a strange coincidence—the death of the one and the rise of the other. I can't imagine, moreover, that Kirov would ever have allowed Beria's election to the Central Committee.

Sergei Kirov was a great friend of the family from way back, probably from their early days in the Caucasus. He knew the Alliluyevs exceedingly well and was very fond of my mother. I have a photograph of Kirov and Yenukidze at my mother's grave. Grief is written all over their faces—the stern faces of two strong men not given to showing their feelings.

After my mother died Kirov would come to see my father at Sochi and they used to take me on outings. I have a pile of photographs taken at about that time, simple family photos with nothing posed about them. They were taken by Vlasik, who accompanied my father on all his trips and who was a good amateur photographer. There I am with the three of us picnicking in the woods; another shows us cruising on a launch not far from shore. Kirov looks relaxed in a long, loose shirt, and my father is wearing a white summer suit. I remember these trips myself. Other people would sometimes come with us, too, perhaps even Beria—I don't remember. But Kirov used to *live* in our house. He was one of us, an old colleague and a friend. My father liked him and was attached to him.

Kirov spent his last summer, that of 1934, with us as in previous years. Then, in December, Nicolayev shot him. Wouldn't it be more logical to link his killing with the name of Beria rather than with that of my father, as is done by transparent hints today?

I'll never believe my father was involved in this particular death. Kirov was closer to him than the Svanidzes, the Redenses, his other relatives, or most of his other colleagues. Kirov was close to my father and my father needed him. I remember when we got the awful news that Kirov was dead, and how shaken everybody was.

Sergo Ordzhonikidze, another of our old friends, died in 1936. I suspect that this, too, was a result of Beria's machinations.

Ordzhonikidze was very close to the family, and his wife Zina was a great friend of my mother's. He used to stay with us at Zubalovo for months at a time. He was a real Georgian— noisy, boisterous and quick to show his feelings. The moment he walked into a room the walls started shaking with his booming voice and loud laughter.

He was well acquainted with Beria from his days in the Caucasus and couldn't stand him. He was also a fairly massive obstacle on Beria's path to power—particularly in Georgia. But as Beria started to rise, Ordzhonikidze's position became very difficult. Aspersions were cast on him in an effort to make bad blood between him and my father. It was too much for him, and in February, 1936, he shot himself. Could he have thought of my mother as he pulled the trigger?

For a long time his death was attributed to medical sabotage. A short time afterward Gorky died. Pletnyov[3] and Levin,[4] the doctors who had treated both of them—Ordzhonikidze had kidney disease—were sent to jail.

When Ordzhonikidze went to Mukholatka in the spring of 1935, he took me along. I remember how he played with me and wanted me with him the whole time. But my hunchbacked governess kept dragging me off somewhere. Ordzhonikidze couldn't stand her any more than I could. Plainly he was taken aback by her and couldn't imagine where on earth they'd ever dug up such a creature.

The grownups on that visit to Mukholatka were Ordzhonikidze, Eikhe,[5] Yezhov and Ordzhonikidze's regular doctor, Izraelit. Professor Pletnyov was there too. Within a year they all came to a terrible end: Eikhe and the doctors were imprisoned and none of them came out alive. At first Yezhov was sending people to jail, but before long he was in jail himself. Ordzhonikidze shot himself. In those years never a month went by in peace. Everything was in constant turmoil. People vanished like shadows in the night. Ehrenburg has given a good description of it. I won't go over it again. At the time I didn't even understand what was going on.

Still a schoolgirl, I saw everything from a different angle. To me these were years of the steady annihilation of everything my mother had created, of systematic elimination of her very spirit so that nothing would be left of it, so that everything would be exactly the opposite of what she had stood for. This is what I could see and understand. This is what I can write about, and I leave the political analysis to others.

Even the deaths of such close friends of my mother's as Bukharin, Kirov and Ordzhonikidze were seen at the time as the destruction of everything that had to do with her. This is how it appeared to the family and the members of the household.

What was the effect of my mother's death? Did it simply leave my father free to do what he would have done in any case? Or was it that her suicide broke his spirit and made him lose his faith in all his old friends? And then—could she have halted the terrible process had she lived?

I doubt it. She, of course, would never have betrayed her old friends. Nothing would ever have convinced her that Yenukidze, her godfather, was an "enemy of the people." But in that case wouldn't she have gone the same way as they did? She would never have been a match for her mortal enemy, Beria.

One can only speculate. I think fate saved her from an ordeal she could never have borne. Maybe it was God himself who spared her that horror. And even had she summoned up strength to leave my father, whom she loved, her fate would have been even worse, because he'd surely have taken his revenge. Didn't she fire her shot, then, out of a logic that was inevitable and profound?

From 1933 until the outbreak of the war, which changed
everybody's life, the whole of my time was divided between
school, the Pioneers,[1] my room at home and my books. It was
a tiny world in which my nurse warmed me like a big Russian
stove. I went to a wonderful school where I made friends and
acquired knowledge and ways of doing things that have stood
me in good stead ever since. I had teachers I'll never forget.
I read a great deal, for my father had a vast library of books
my mother had started collecting and there was no one to read
them but me. As for my nurse, with her gentleness and kindness, her sense of humor and happy disposition, she and the
love she gave me made a sort of "air cushion" around me. It
was my protection against the world outside, against everything that was happening. Not only was I wrapped in cotton

wool right up to the time I entered the university, not only was I behind the fortress wall, but I was in the special atmosphere my nurse had created in the two rooms we lived in together, where I would sit at my table working and she at hers, reading or sewing. Where we were it was quiet. We weren't even aware that everything around us was being shattered.

My nurse did everything she knew how to preserve the atmosphere created by my mother, an atmosphere of study and work and healthy play in the out-of-doors. It was she who preserved my childhood. How often I think of her, and how I thank her for it!

Until war broke out in Europe my father and I used to see each other often. Those are the years that left me with the memory that he loved me and tried to be a father to me and bring me up the best he knew how. All this collapsed when the war came. As I grew older there were conflicts and differences of opinion. But in those years I loved him tenderly, as he loved me. He used to say I was like his mother. That touched him, I think.

My nurse brought me up in unquestioning love of and obedience to my father. Whatever else might be going on, that was an inviolable law of Christian conduct as far as she was concerned.

My father came to dinner every night. Before he'd even taken off his overcoat he'd come down the corridor past my room and shout, "Housekeeper!" I'd put down my homework and rush to the dining room, a big room lined with bookshelves. There was a large, carved sideboard with my mother's cups on it and a table with the latest newspapers and magazines. Above it was a large portrait of my mother, a blown-up print of one of the photographs taken at our house. The table would be set for the usual eight. I would sit on my father's right. It was generally seven in the evening. We were usually at the table for two hours. I just listened while the grownups did the talking. After a while my father would ask how I'd done in school that day. Since my marks were excellent until I got to the eighth grade, he was always very proud. They'd all sing my praises and send me off to bed.

My father would leave late to spend the night at Kuntsevo. Sometimes before he left he'd come to my room in his overcoat to kiss me good night as I lay sleeping. He liked kissing me while I was little, and I'll never forget how tender he was to me. It was the warm Georgian tenderness to children.

It was in these years that my father started taking me to movies and the theater. The ones we went to most often were the Moscow Art Theater, the Maly, the Bolshoi and the Vakhtangov. We saw *The Hot Heart, Yegor Bulychov, Lyubov Yarovaya* and *Platon Krechet.* And we heard *Boris Godunov, Sadko* and *Ivan Susanin* at the opera. My father went to the theater a good deal before the war. Usually we went in a group. They'd put me in the front row of the box. My father would sit somewhere way in back.

But the movies were what thrilled me most of all. There was a theater in the Kremlin, on the site of what had once been the Winter Garden, with passageways linking it to the old Kremlin Palace. We used to go after dinner, about nine in the evening. It was late for me, of course, but I begged so hard that my father couldn't refuse. He'd push me in front and say with a laugh, "You show us how to get there, House-keeper. Without you to guide us we'd never find it!" I'd lead a whole long procession to the other end of the deserted Kremlin. Behind us came the many members of the body-guard and the heavy armored cars crawling at a snail's pace. We generally saw two movies, maybe more, and stayed till two in the morning. I'd be sent home to bed and be up at seven the next day for school.

My governess objected and told me I ought to refuse when I was invited at such a late hour. But how could I possibly refuse? So many wonderful movies were shown for the first time on the little screen in the Kremlin! There were *Chapayev,* the Gorky trilogy, films about Peter the Great, *Circus* and *Volga-Volga.* All the best Soviet films were launched in that hall in the Kremlin. At first it was Zakhar Shumyatsky who used to present them to the government. Later it was Dukelsky and later, for many years, I. G. Bolshakov.

In those days, before the war, it wasn't yet the custom for the Party to criticize films and insist that they be remade. They were seen, approved and then released for public distribution. Even if something wasn't quite right, nothing happened to the movie or those who had made it. It was only after the war that it became customary to denounce nearly every new film that was made.

I'd get out of the movie late and go racing home through the empty, quiet Kremlin. The next day at school I could think of nothing but the heroes I'd seen on film the night before.

My father thought it was better for me to watch movies than to sit at home. Possibly he didn't even think whether it would be better for me or not. Maybe he just liked having me along. I amused and diverted him, and was a comfort to him besides.

Sometimes after school was out in the summer he'd take me to Kuntsevo for three days or so. He enjoyed having me around. But it didn't work out because it was impossible for anybody to fit in with his way of life. He'd have his first meal at two or three in the afternoon and dinner at eight in the evening. Then he'd sit up late at the table. I wasn't used to it.

It was too much for me. The one thing I liked was our walks in the garden and woods. He'd ask me the names of various flowers and grasses and what sort of bird was that singing? All this was lore I had learned from my nurse. But then he'd sit down in the shade somewhere with his newspapers and official documents and begin reading. At that point he didn't need me any more. I'd get restless and bored and long to leave as quickly as possible for Zubalovo, where I could take one of my friends to stay with me and there were so many things I enjoyed.

Meantime my father thought it was being with him that bored me, and that hurt his feelings. We had one quarrel that lasted quite a while. I asked him straight out, "May I go away now?" "Go," came the brusque reply. After that he didn't speak to me or call me up for a long time. It wasn't until I asked his forgiveness under the prodding of my wise old nurse that he was willing to make up. I heard him mutter angrily, "She went away! Imagine leaving her old father like that! Says she's bored!" But he was kissing me and had already forgiven me, for without me he had been lonelier than ever.

Sometimes he appeared unexpectedly at Zubalovo, which, however deserted and greatly changed it was, was still infinitely precious to us all. Grandfather and Grandmother would both come down from their rooms. Someone would telephone Zubalovo Two. Mikoyan might come over, or Uncle Pavel would appear quickly with the children. Then we'd all have a picnic in the woods. There'd be a table, and shashlik sizzling over a fire, and everyone would have an excellent light Georgian wine. My father used to send me to the poultry yard for guinea and pheasant eggs. They were easy to find in the spaces underneath the bushes, and the grownups would cook them in the hot ashes. We children generally had a good time on these picnics, but I'm not so sure about the grownups.

One time Grandmother wept loudly and my father went away angry and upset. The grownups had dealt each other too many wounds and had too many reasons to be unhappy with one another.

Grandfather always did his best to smooth things over and calm everybody down. Grandmother, on the other hand, liked to have things out in the open. They'd scold each other for a long time after my father had gone.

Zubalovo was changed under our very eyes. First they painted the house. Then they dug up the enormous old lilacs that used to bloom beside the terrace like two huge, sweet-smelling haystacks and carted them off. Next they took away the old bird-cherry thickets on the ground that they were insect breeders and it wasn't good having them next to the vegetable garden. Then they covered the marvelous level sandy roads with hideous gray asphalt.

All these things were done by the commandants, the men who ran the place. They worked zealously to make everything exactly the way it was at my father's at Kuntsevo. A few fir trees had only to be planted at Kuntsevo for there to be an uproar at Zubalovo. Lo and behold, there'd be fir trees all over the place. But it was dry and sandy at Zubalovo and the fir trees quickly shriveled and died. We were so pleased!

The servants, state employees every one, treated us as if we didn't even exist. Besides, they were changed so often they never had a chance to get used to us, or we to them. Since the "boss," moreover, didn't live there and didn't seem to care much about us, they didn't bother to be polite.

On account of their lack of courtesy Grandmother was forever making scenes for which they disliked her even more than the rest of us. Grandfather would scold and try to make her see that she didn't "understand." "You're quite right," Grandmother would exclaim. "There are some things I'll never understand!" With that she'd flounce off to her room, muttering about "lazy good-for-nothings."

Once, continuing one of her quarrels with Grandfather, she screamed loudly in my direction, "Your mother was a fool, a fool! How many times did I tell her she was a fool, but she wouldn't listen! She paid for it, too!" I started to cry and yelled, "You're a fool yourself!" I ran to my nurse for moral support. I remembered my mother and I loved the memory of her. Until I was sixteen I believed what the grownups told me, that she had died of appendicitis, and I couldn't bear to hear an unkind word about her.

Without her, the family at Zubalovo started squabbling, a thing that never happened while she was alive. Uncle Fyodor, who stayed there from time to time, quarreled with my older brother Yakov, who was living there with his wife. Yakov didn't get along with Vasily. Although they were brothers, they were so different they could never agree on anything. Yakov's wife was at odds with my grandparents. And my grandparents bickered with one another. Pavel's wife, who became his widow in 1938, appeared and she, too, had a sharp tongue that only made matters worse. We children spun back and forth, taking first one side, then the other, and never really knowing what was going on. My nurse was a born peacemaker and always managed to keep on splendid terms with everyone. As a result she was forever being entrusted with diplomatic errands to smooth things over.

No, it wasn't the same at Zubalovo any more. The spirit was altogether different—the spirit and the entire setting. All the hostile factions sought my father's support. They enlisted me. "Go tell Papa" such-and-such. I went, but my father told me off. "Why do you repeat everything they tell you like an empty drum?" He ordered me not to dare come to him any more with requests on behalf of others. Sometimes at school people gave me letters for him. He ordered me not to bring letters from anybody or serve as a "post office box."

Sometimes when my father went to Sochi in the summer, he sent me and my nurse to Mukholatka, in the Crimea. I still have a lot of letters my father sent me from Sochi, or to me at Sochi or the Crimea.

Here are a few excerpts:

HELLO MY LITTLE SPARROW!

Don't be angry with me for not answering right away. I was very busy. I'm alive and well. I feel fine.

I give my little sparrow a big hug.

MY DEAR SETANKA!

I got your letter of September 25. Thank you for not forgetting your little papa. I'm all right. I'm well, but I miss you. Did you get the peaches and pomegranates? I'll send you some more if you order me to. Tell Vasya to write me, too. Good-bye, then. I give you a big kiss.

YOUR LITTLE PAPA

Thank you for your letter, my Setanochka.

I'm sending you peaches, fifty for you and fifty for Vasya. Write me if you need some more peaches or some other kinds of fruit. I'll send them. I give you a kiss.

September 8, 1934

LITTLE HOUSEKEEPER!

I got your letter and postcard. I'm glad you haven't forgotten your little papa. I'm sending you a few red apples. In a few days I'll send tangerines. Eat them and enjoy yourself. I'm not sending Vasya any because he's doing badly in school. The weather is nice here. Only, I'm lonely because my Housekeeper isn't with me. All the best, then, my little Housekeeper. I give you a big kiss.

October 8, 1935

SETANKA AND VASYA!

I'm sending you some sweets that my mother, your grand-mother, just sent me from Tiflis. Go halves and don't fight about it. Treat anyone you want.

April 18, 1935

HELLO, LITTLE HOUSEKEEPER!

I'm sending you pomegranates, tangerines and some candied fruit. Eat and enjoy them, my little Housekeeper! I'm not send-ing any to Vasya because he's still doing badly at school and feeds me nothing but promises. Tell him I don't believe promises made in words and that I'll believe Vasya only when he really starts to study, even if his marks are only "good." I report to you, Comrade Housekeeper, that I was in Tiflis for one day. I was at my mother's and I gave her regards from you and Vasya. She is well, more or less, and she gives both of you a big kiss. Well, that's all right now. I give you a kiss. I'll see you soon.

October 18, 1935

HELLO, MY LITTLE HOUSEKEEPER!

I got your letter. Thank you! I am well. I'm getting on all right. Vasya had a sore throat but he's better now. Am I going to go south? I was planning to, but I don't dare budge from this spot without an order from you. I've been at Lipki a lot. It's hot here. How are you in the Crimea? I kiss my little sparrow.

HELLO, MY LITTLE SPARROW!

I got your letter. Thank you for the fish. Only, I beg you, little Housekeeper, don't send me any more fish. If you like it in the Crimea, you can stay at Mukholatka all summer. I give you a big kiss. Your little papa.

July 7, 1938

GREETINGS TO MY HOUSEKEEPER, SETANKA!

I got all your letters. Thank you for the letters! I didn't answer the letters because I was very busy. What are you up to, how is your English, and how are you? I am healthy and in good spirits as always. It's a bit lonely without you, but what can I do? I'll be patient. I give my little Housekeeper a kiss.

July 22, 1939

HELLO, MY LITTLE HOUSEKEEPER!

I got both your letters. I'm glad you haven't forgotten your little papa. I couldn't answer you right away. I was busy.

I hear you weren't alone at Ritsa[2] and that you had a young man with you. Well, there's nothing wrong with that. Ritsa is nice, especially if you have a young man along, my little sparrow.

When do you mean to set out for Moscow? Isn't it time? I think so. Come to Moscow by August 25, or even the twentieth. Write me what you think of this. I don't plan to come south this year. I'm busy. I can't get away. My health? I'm well. My spirits are good. I miss you a bit, but you'll be coming soon.

I give you a big hug, my little sparrow.

August 8, 1939

My father signed all his letters to me exactly the same way: "From Setanka-Housekeeper's wretched Secretary, the poor peasant J. Stalin." I guess I'd better explain.

In the game my father thought up, as I've told you, he used to call me "Housekeeper," and he and all the colleagues he used to bring home nearly every day were my "Secretaries" or "Wretched Secretaries." I've no idea whether it amused the rest of them or not, but my father kept it up until the war. I answered in the same vein and sent him "orders" like the one below. He thought up the form of these, too.

Oct. 21, 1934   To Comrade J. V. Stalin
                                                            Secretary No. 1
                            Order No. 4
                 I order you to take me with you.
                                         Signed: SETANKA-HOUSEKEEPER
                                                            Seal.
Signed: Secretary No. 1   I submit.   J. STALIN

Apparently they'd forgotten to take me with them to the theater or a movie on some occasion or other and I was asking them to take me next time. One time it was: "I order you to let me go to Zubalovo tomorrow. —May 10, 1934." Another time: "I order you to take me to the theater with you. —April 15, 1934." Still another: "I order you to let me go to the movies. Ask them to show *Chapayev* and an American comedy. —Oct. 28, 1934."

Under the order my father would write "I obey," or "I submit," or "Agreed," or "It will be done."

Since my father was forever requesting new "orders" and I was getting tired of it, I once sent him this appeal: "I order you to permit me to send you an order only once a week. — Feb. 26, 1937."

When I got older I varied my demands a little: "Papa! Seeing that it's freezing outside, I order you to wear your fur overcoat. Setanka-Housekeeper. —Dec. 15, 1938."

Another time, when he came home so late I couldn't wait up, I left a message by his place at the table:

MY DEAR LITTLE PAPA!

I'm resorting once again to the old and tried method of writing you a message since I can't wait up.

You may eat and drink—though not a lot—and talk.

Your late arrival, Comrade Secretary, compels me to give you a reprimand.

Finally, I give my little papa a big kiss and ask him to come earlier in the future.

SETANKA-HOUSEKEEPER

The message was dated October 11, 1940. My father wrote across it: "To my little sparrow. I read this with pleasure. Little papa."

The last humorous message I wrote to him is dated May, 1941, on the eve of the war.

MY DEAR LITTLE SECRETARY,

I hasten to inform you that your Housekeeper got an "excellent" in her composition! Thus, she passed the first test and has another tomorrow. Eat and drink to your heart's content. I send my little papa a thousand kisses. Greetings to the secretaries.

HOUSEKEEPER

A "minute" was written across the top of this one: "We send greetings to our Housekeeper! On behalf of the secretaries—little papa J. Stalin."

The war started soon after that and no one was in the mood for games and jokes any more. But my nickname "Setanka-Housekeeper" stuck, and for years, long after I was grown up, everyone who used to play the game called me "Housekeeper"[3] and remembered the "orders" I used to issue as a child.

I was fifteen when the war started. We were sent to Kuibyshev in the fall of 1941 and I spent my ninth-grade year there. Events that occurred about that time, in 1942 and 1943, came between me and my father permanently. We began to become alienated from one another. But I shall never forget his affection, his love and tenderness to me as a child. He was rarely as tender to anyone as he was to me. At one time he must have loved my mother very much. And he also loved and respected his own mother.

He said she was an intelligent woman. He was thinking of the quality of her mind and not her education, since she was hardly able to write her own name. Sometimes he'd tell us how she used to spank him when he was little and how she used to hit his father when he drank too much.* Apparently she had a strict, decisive character. My father was delighted by

---

* His father died in a drunken brawl after being stabbed with a knife.

that. She was left a widow young, and that caused her to become more severe.

She had had a great many children, but they all died in early childhood and my father was the only one who survived. She was extremely devout and dreamed of having her son become a priest. She kept her religion to the end of her days. When my father went to see her shortly before she died, she told him, "What a pity you never became a priest."

My father used to recount this with relish. He was delighted by her scorn for what he'd accomplished, for the acclaim and the worldly glory.

She never wanted to leave Georgia and come to live in Moscow, though my father and mother both asked her. She had no use for life in the capital. She preferred to go on living her quiet, unpretentious life as a simple, pious old woman. She was about eighty when she died in 1936. My father was deeply upset and spoke about her for years afterward.

But he was a bad and neglectful son, as he was a father and husband. He devoted his whole being to something else, to politics and struggle. And so people who weren't personally close were always more important to him than those who were.

As a rule my father didn't nag or find fault with me. His guidance as a parent was of the most general sort—that I should study hard, be out in the fresh air as much as possible, and that I ought not to be given in to or spoiled.

From time to time my father indulged in a bit of petty carping. It was painful, but it didn't happen often. Once in Sochi when I was ten he glanced at me (I was a rather big child) and remarked, "What's this, are you going around naked?" I had no idea what the matter might be. "It's that," he went on, pointing at the hem of my dress. It was above the knees, the normal length for a child of my age. "To hell with it"—he was angry by now. "What's that?" This time it was my shorts. "These girls who go in for sport! What an outrage!" He was getting angrier by the minute. "They all go around naked!" He went off to his room and came back with two cotton undershirts. "Come on," he commanded me. "Here, nurse," he said to my nurse, whose face registered no surprise whatsoever. "You make her some bloomers to cover up her knees. And see that her dress is *below* the knees!" "Certainly, certainly," answered my nurse, who had never quarreled with an employer in her life. "But, Papa," I wailed, "nobody wears them that way now!"

That was no reason as far as he was concerned. They made me a pair of long, foolish-looking bloomers and a dress that came below my knees, and I only wore them when I was going to see my father. Later I shortened the dress little by little and he never noticed, because his mind was on other things. I soon went back to dressing exactly as I had before.

But he drove me to tears more than once with his nagging over what I wore. I had only to be wearing socks instead of stockings in the summertime for him to scold me, without warning: "Going around with bare legs again, I see." He insisted that I wear dresses that hung on me like sacks and weren't nipped in at the waist. Or he'd rip the beret off my head with a "What sort of pancake is that? Can't you find yourself a better-looking hat than that?" No matter how many times I told him girls were wearing berets now, he wouldn't budge. In his day girls wore hats, and that was all there was to it.

Later I learned from Alexandra Nakashidze that in Georgia older people don't tolerate short dresses, short sleeves or socks.

Even when I was grown up, every time I was going to see my father I had to stop and think whether the colors I was wearing were too bright, since he was bound to take me to task. "You can't imagine what you look like," he'd tell me sometimes, without thinking who else might be present. Maybe he resented the fact that I didn't look like my mother and was stuck in the awkward, adolescent stage for what seemed an uncommonly long time. Something was obviously wrong with my looks as far as he was concerned. And it wasn't long before my mental outlook began bothering him, too.

Once the war started, even our infrequent meetings came to an end, and he and I drifted apart. After the war we were never really close again. I had grown up. My childish games and amusements, which had been a diversion to him once, were now a thing of the far-off past.

➤➤➤ *14*

The war broke out on June 22, 1941. My oldest brother Yakov left for the front the next day with his battery and his graduating class at the Frunze Military Academy. They finished just in time to go to war.

He never took advantage of who he was, never made the slightest attempt to avoid danger—to be assigned to the rear or to a headquarters behind the battle lines, even to get out of being sent to Belorussia, the worst part of the front.

Everything about him, his character and his entire scrupulous, honorable, incorruptible approach to life, precluded any such thing. Since my father, moreover, had no use for him and everybody knew it, no one in the higher echelons of the army gave him special treatment. My father would only have been furious.

It seemed inappropriate for Yakov to become a professional soldier, for he was peace-loving at heart, gentle, a little slow-moving and extremely quiet, though firm and resolute within. In looks, except for his almond-shaped eyes, he did not resemble my father. He looked more like his mother, Yekaterina Svanidze, who died when he was two years old. It was a striking resemblance, to judge by her photographs. He must have inherited his character from her, too, for there was nothing rough or abrasive or fanatical about him. He wasn't ambitious and he couldn't have cared less about power. His qualities were in harmony with one another, as were the things he wanted out of life. He wasn't brilliant, but he was simple, unassuming, hard-working and capable. He had a quiet charm.

I saw him angry only twice. Otherwise I never would have known he was capable of anger. Both times his loss of temper was occasioned by Vasily's penchant for profanity in front of me and other women, and in general for swearing whenever he felt like it, no matter who happened to be present. Yakov couldn't stand it. He turned on Vasily like a lion and they had a fist fight.

Yakov spent his early years in Tbilisi. His mother's sister Sashiko brought him up. He came to Moscow to study as a young man at the urging of his Uncle Alexander Svanidze. My father didn't want him there, but my mother tried to keep an eye on him. He had a very hard time, living in the apartment in the Kremlin with the rest of us and trying to learn Russian, which didn't come easily to him at first. Very likely he'd have been happier and better off with his cousins in Georgia.

Yakov always felt like a stepchild with my father, but not with my mother, whose stepson he actually was. He loved her very much. His first marriage was a tragic one. My father didn't even want to hear about the marriage, much less help.

He bullied Yakov and picked on him. Yakov shot himself one
night in the kitchen next to his little room. The bullet passed
right through him, but he was ill for a long time. My nurse
later told me that after this my father treated him worse than
before, heaping contempt on him for being a "weakling."

After his recovery Yakov went to live in Grandfather Alliluyev's apartment in Leningrad. He and his wife had a
daughter whom he adored, but she died in infancy. The first
marriage was a failure and soon broke up. Yakov was an electri-
cal engineer and worked at a Leningrad power station. If only
he could have stayed in this peaceful line of work!

Yakov came back to Moscow in 1935 and entered the Frunze
Academy. A year or so later he married a very fine woman
who had been abandoned by her husband. Yulia was Jewish,
and that displeased my father, too. He never liked Jews,
though he wasn't as blatant about expressing his hatred for
them in those days as he was after the war.

But Yakov stood firm. Though he knew all Yulia's weaknesses and inadequacies, he chivalrously stood up for her
whenever anybody criticized her. He loved her and their
daughter Gulia, who was born in 1938. He was a fine husband
and father, and he ignored my father's patent disapproval of
his choice.

Sometimes Yakov appeared at our apartment in the Kremlin
and played with me or watched me doing my homework as he
waited tensely for my father to arrive. He usually sat at the
table in silence. Yakov respected our father's judgment and
opinions. It was at his wish that Yakov chose to become a
soldier. But they were too unlike each other ever to be com-
patible. "Father speaks in ready-made formulas," Yakov complained to me once. Yakov's gentleness and composure were
irritating to my father, who was quick-tempered and impetu-
ous even in his later years.

Yakov and his family stayed with us at Zubalovo every

summer until the war broke out. We studied together each spring, he getting ready for his examinations and I for mine. My father had built a Russian bath at Zubalovo. He had learned to like them in Siberia and taught us to enjoy them, too. Above the bath there was a large attic where dry birch branches hung. The attic was fragrant and dry. We spread a rug out on the floor and did our studying there. I was fifteen and Yakov thirty-three when the war started, and we had only just become real friends. I loved him because he was so gentle, even-tempered and quiet. He always loved me and played with me. Later on I played with his daughter just as he used to play with me. If it hadn't been for the war, we'd have been the best of friends all our lives.

Yakov left for the front the day after it started. We said good-bye over the phone, as there was no time to see one another before he left. His unit was sent directly to where the chaos was worst, near Baranovichi in western Belorussia. Soon there was no news at all.

Yulia and Gulia stayed with us. I've no idea why (in the first months of the war no one, not even my father, had any clear idea what to do), but we were all sent to Sochi: my grandfather and grandmother, Anna Redens and her two sons, Yulia and Gulia and my nurse and I. At the end of August I talked to my father on the telephone from Sochi. Yulia was next to me, and never took her eyes off me the whole time. I asked why we hadn't heard from Yakov. Slowly and distinctly he uttered the words, "Yasha has been taken prisoner." Before I could open my mouth he added, "Don't say anything to his wife for the time being." Yulia could see from my face that something was wrong and started asking me questions the moment I put down the phone. I just kept repeating over and over again, "He doesn't know anything himself." I was so stricken by the news that I couldn't bear to break it to Yulia. Let somebody else do it.

But the considerations that guided my father weren't so humane. Somehow he'd gotten the idea that someone had "tricked" Yakov and "betrayed" him intentionally. Mightn't Yulia have been a party to it? When we got back to Moscow that September he told me, "Yasha's daughter can stay with you awhile. But it seems that his wife is dishonest. We'll have to look into it."

So Yulia was arrested in Moscow in the fall of 1941 and was in prison until the spring of 1943 when it "turned out" she'd had nothing to do with Yakov's capture and when his conduct as a prisoner finally convinced my father that he hadn't surrendered on purpose.

During the autumn of 1941 leaflets with Yakov's photograph were dropped on Moscow. He looked dark and thin. He was in his uniform, without his belt or officer's epaulets. Vasily brought some leaflets home. We examined them a long time, hoping they were forgeries. But no, it was Yakov all right.

Years later many former prisoners of war returned home from Soviet camps in Siberia or the Far North, where they had been sent as soon as they came back from Germany. A lot of them had heard about Yakov's being a prisoner of war, since the Germans used this fact for propaganda. They also knew that his conduct had been honorable. He had refused to lend himself to the Germans' efforts at provocation and had been subjected to cruel treatment as a result.

After Stalingrad, in the winter of 1943-44, my father said to me suddenly during one of our rare meetings, "The Germans have proposed that we exchange one of their prisoners for Yasha. They want me to make a deal with them! I won't do it. War is war." I could tell by his tone that he was upset. He wouldn't say another word about it and just shoved something in English under my nose, something from his correspondence with Roosevelt, with the words: "Translate!

Here you've been studying all this English. Can you translate anything?" I translated it, to his pleasure and surprise, and the audience was over, since he had no more time for me.

He spoke to me about Yakov again in the summer of 1945, when the war was already over. We hadn't seen each other in a long time. "The Germans shot Yasha. I had a letter of condolence from a Belgian officer, Prince somebody or other. He was an eyewitness. The Americans set them all free." He spoke with an effort and didn't want to say any more.

Valentina Istomina, or Valechka, who was my father's housekeeper at the time, told me later that Voroshilov heard a similar story about Yakov's death in Germany at the very end of the war. He suffered over it, for Voroshilov, like everyone who knew him, loved my brother, and didn't know how to tell my father. So they heard it from two separate sources.*

Maybe when Yakov was dead and it was too late, my father felt some warmth for him at last and realized he had been unfair. Yakov was a prisoner for four years, which he must have found harder to bear than anybody else. He was a quiet hero. His heroism was as selfless, honorable and unassuming as the whole of his life had been.

Recently in a French magazine I came across an article by a Scots officer who purported to be another eyewitness of Yakov's death. You have to be skeptical about articles like that because so many false things have appeared in the West about the "private life" of my father and the various members of his family. Two things, however, make the article appear authentic. One is a photograph of Yakov looking thin and emaciated and wearing a soldier's overcoat. It is undoubtedly genuine. The other is the fact that the author cites my father as answering in the negative when some newspaper corre-

* It is difficult to say whether these sources are reliable. I think Yakov's death is still a mystery.

spondents formally inquired whether his son was a prisoner or not. He pretended not to know it, in other words, and thereby abandoned Yakov to his fate. It was very like my father to wash his hands of the members of his own family, to wipe them out of his mind and act as if they didn't exist. We betrayed all our prisoners the same way, though.

Yakov's life, in any case, was always upright and honest. He was unassuming and loathed any mention of who he was. He was steadfast and honorable in refusing privileges and never received any.

Later there was an attempt to immortalize him as a hero. My father told me that when the director Mikhail Chiaureli was making the movie that turned out to be the lifeless spectacular *The Fall of Berlin,* he approached my father about an idea he had of showing Yakov as a war hero. Chiaureli was a hack who sensed that he could exploit Yakov's tragic story. My father didn't give his consent, and I think he was right. Chiaureli would have made the same sort of false puppet out of Yakov that he did out of everybody else. He wanted Yakov's story only so he could exalt my father, a thing he relished. Thank God Yakov wasn't shown in such a guise.

Justice to Yakov was the last thing my father had in mind, of course, in turning Chiaureli down. He was merely unwilling to thrust his relatives to the fore because he considered every one of them without exception to be unworthy of being so commemorated.

No one deserves to be remembered with greater gratitude than Yakov. What greater heroism in our day than to be an honest and upright man?

⤷ 15

When the war broke out, a sense of community was awakened in people. Differences in outlook fell away in the face of common danger.

It was so even in our shattered family. As I've mentioned already, we were all sent to Sochi—my grandmother, grandfather, Yakov's daughter Gulia and her mother, my Aunt Anna and her children, my nurse and I. When we got back to Moscow in September, we found that a corner of the Arsenal Building opposite our windows had been destroyed by a bomb. They were hurrying to finish a bomb shelter for members of the government in front of our house. It was to have a passageway from the apartment we lived in. I was in the shelter with my father on several occasions.

Life was in turmoil and there was nothing that didn't

frighten us. We had to leave Moscow and go to school somewhere else. A bomb fell on our school, and that was frighten-
ing, too.

Then—and this, too, was unexpected—they gathered us up
and packed us off to Kuibyshev. It took them a long time load-
ing all our belongings onto a special van. Nobody knew
whether my father would be going there from Moscow or not,
but they loaded his library just to be on the safe side.

In Kuibyshev we were all assigned to a small building with
a little courtyard of its own on Pioneer Street. It was a museum
that had been converted in a great hurry. The whole place
still smelled of paint and the corridors of mice as well. Our
whole retinue came with us: Alexandra Nakashidze and all
the cooks, waitresses and bodyguards, right up to and including my nurse and my secret police "watchdog," Mikhail Klimov. Vasily's first wife came, too. She was a nice young girl
named Galya. She was pregnant, and in October, 1941, gave
birth to a son, Sasha, in Kuibyshev. Room was somehow made
for everyone in our new dwelling place. Grandmother even
kept squabbling with Alexandra Nakashidze as usual. Grandfather was the only one who wasn't there. He preferred to be
in Tbilisi. He went there straight from Sochi and spent two
splendid years in Georgia.

The house was full to bursting. I went to school and was in
the ninth grade; we listened there to the news every day over
the radio. The autumn of 1941 was a very anxious time.

In late October I went to Moscow to see my father. He didn't
write and it was difficult to talk with him over the phone because he got tense and angry and kept saying he didn't have
time to talk.

I got to Moscow on October 28, the day bombs were dropped
on the Bolshoi Theater, the university buildings on Mokho-
vaya Street and the Central Committee building on Staraya

Ploshchad. My father was in the Kremlin shelter, and I went there to join him. The rooms were wood-paneled exactly like Kuntsevo and the furniture was exactly the same. The commandants took pride in the fact that they had copied the house in Kuntsevo so closely and felt sure that in this way they were pleasing my father. There was the same long table set for dinner, with the same people there as always, except that now they were all in uniform. They were in a state of high excitement because of the small bombs that a Nazi reconnaissance plane had been dropping all over Moscow.

My father didn't notice me—I was only in the way. There were maps on the tables and on all the walls, and he was receiving reports on the situation at the front line.

Finally he caught sight of me and had to say something. "How are you getting on there? Have you made friends with anybody in Kuibyshev?" he asked casually.

"No," I said. "They've set up a special school there for children who've been evacuated, and there's a whole lot of them." It never occurred to me that this remark might cause any special reaction.

My father suddenly turned a pair of darting eyes on me as he always did when something made him mad. "What? A special school?" I saw that he was getting angrier by the minute. "Ah, you—" he was trying to find a word that wasn't too improper—"Ah, you damned caste! Just think! The government and the people from Moscow come and they give them their own school. That scoundrel Vlasik—I bet he's behind it!" By this time he was furious and was distracted only because there were pressing matters to attend to and other people in the room.

He was quite right. It was a caste, a caste of bigwigs from the capital that had come to Kuibyshev. Half the population had to be evicted to make room for all these families, who were used to a comfortable life and felt cramped in modest provincial apartments.

But it was too late to do anything about it. The caste was already in existence, and it lived by laws of its own.

It was quite evident in Kuibyshev, where the people from Moscow were stewing in their own juice. Our evacuee school really was full of the children of well-known Moscow people. It was so distilled a group and so awesome a spectacle that some of the local teachers were too intimidated even to go into the classroom. I spent only one year there, thank heaven, and went back to Moscow in June.

I visited Moscow in November, 1941, and in January, 1942, for a day or two each time, to see my father. He was just as irritable and busy as on my first visit and had absolutely no time for me and my foolish, domestic concerns.

I felt terribly alone that winter. Maybe it was my age—sixteen, a time of dreams and doubts and seeking unlike anything I'd ever known before. It was in Kuibyshev that I first started listening to serious music. There were concerts given by a philharmonic orchestra made up of musicians who'd been evacuated from Moscow, and it was there that Shostakovich's Seventh Symphony was performed for the first time.

In a long, dark corridor downstairs next to the kitchen of our house was a place where movies were shown. There we used to look at newsreels from the front: Leningrad under siege, the autumn battles outside Moscow and so on. The newsreels of those years were unforgettable. They were filmed in battle, in the trenches, under advancing tanks.

Vasily came for a brief visit to see his son. He had graduated from the Lipetsk Aviation Institute just before the war and afterward flew fighter planes. But he was already a major and had been appointed Inspector in Chief of the Air Force. Nobody really knew what his job was, but he was directly subordinate to my father. Vasily spent a short time near Orel. Then his headquarters were shifted to Moscow and he had an enormous office on Pirogov Street. In Kuibyshev he was surrounded by pilots whom none of us knew. They fawned over him, and he wasn't yet twenty years old. He was later ruined by this fawning and currying of favor. Not one of the old friends who'd been on an equal footing with him was there. All these people were courting him. Their wives came to call on Galya and tried to cultivate her as well.

The house was always full. Everything was in confusion, on the outside and inside—in our heads—as well. There was no one, no one at all, to whom I could open my heart, no one who could teach me anything or help me with a firm, honest word.

I made a terrible discovery that winter. I used to read English and American magazines like *Life, Fortune* and the *Illustrated London News,* both for the information they contained and to practice reading English. One day I came across an article about my father. It mentioned, not as news but as a fact well known to everyone, that his wife, Nadezhda Sergeyevna Alliluyeva, had killed herself on the night of November 8, 1932.

I was shocked and couldn't believe my eyes. But the terrible thing is that in my heart I believed it because everything had been so unlikely at the time.

I rushed to Grandmother and told her, "I know everything. Why did you hide it from me?" Grandmother was extremely surprised and immediately started filling in the details of how it had happened. "Who would have thought it?" she repeated over and over again. "Who would have thought she'd ever have done such a thing?"

From that moment on I had no peace. I tried to remember everything I could. I thought about my father and what he was like and about the fact that he really was hard to get along with. I kept wondering why, why, and no one would give me a clear explanation. Besides, Grandmother and Aunt Anna hadn't really understood my mother that well. As far as they were concerned the event had been pushed into the background by other, newer misfortunes like the deaths of Uncle Pavel, Redens and both the Svanidzes. Time had dulled their memories and their pain.

The whole thing nearly drove me out of my mind. Something in me was destroyed. I was no longer able to obey the word and will of my father and defer to his opinions without question.

Yakov's wife Yulia had vanished just before we left Moscow. People said she'd been arrested on suspicion of "betraying" him to the Germans. The words my father had told me over the telephone—"Don't say anything to Yasha's wife for the time being"—and everything else connected with Yulia's recent arrest began to seem strange to me.

I started wondering about something that had never occurred to me before; namely, was my father always right after all? It was blasphemy even to think such a thing then. In the eyes of everyone around me my father's name was linked with the will to win the war, with the hope of victory and an end to the war. And my father himself was so remote, so incredibly far away. These were my first feeble stirrings of doubt.

Preparations were made for my father to come to Kuibyshev, too, during the autumn of 1941. Several *dachas* were made ready for him on the banks of the Volga and huge air-raid shelters were built underground. What had been the building of the provincial committee of the Communist Party was set aside for him in town, and they fixed exactly the same kind of empty rooms with sofas and tables as he had in Moscow. All this was kept in readiness all winter.

Finally in June, 1942, I went back to Moscow with my

nurse, Vasily's wife and child and Alexandra Nakashidze. I was determined not to leave Moscow again no matter what.

I was greatly distressed to find that Zubalovo had been blown up in the autumn when the Germans had been expected any moment. We went out to see for ourselves. The thick old walls stood there like ugly shells. A new house was being built that was a simplified version of the old one and not the least bit like it. Something had been lost beyond recall. For the time being we settled in one of the wings. By October we were able to move into the newly completed house. It was an absurd, hideous thing. It had been painted dark green for camouflage. The tower and terraces looked truncated compared with what they'd been before. Heaven only knows how to describe it! All of us settled in there, Vasily with his wife and child, Yakov's daughter Gulia and her nurse, my nurse and I, Anna Redens and her sons.

Life at Zubalovo was unpleasant and out of the ordinary that winter of 1942-43. There was an atmosphere of drunkenness and debauchery that never had been there before. Various guests came to see Vasily—famous athletes, actors and pilots who were friends of his. A tremendous amount of drinking went on all the time. The record player was going constantly, and the revelry went on as if there were no war. Yet at the same time it was terribly lonely. There wasn't a soul with whom I could have a serious conversation about what was actually going on in the world and in our country, much less what was going on inside me. I was used to its being boring at home, to isolation and loneliness. But at least it had been boring and quiet. Now it was boring and noisy.

In August of 1942 Winston Churchill came to Moscow. One day Alexandra Nakashidze telephoned and told me I was to come into town. Churchill was having dinner in our apartment that night and my father had given orders that I was to be home. I went in wondering whether it would be all right to say a few words of English or better simply to remain quiet.

Our apartment was empty and depressing. My father's library was in Kuibyshev, and the bookshelves in the dining room were empty. Someone had telephoned from the Ministry of Foreign Affairs to explain the etiquette for dealing with foreigners, and the servants were fussing anxiously around.

Finally they all came down the corridor and went into the dining room. I followed. My father was in an unusually cordial frame of mind. He was in one of those amiable and hospitable moods when he could charm anybody. Patting me on the head, he said, "This is my daughter," and added, "She's a redhead!" Churchill smiled and remarked that he had been red-haired, too, when he was a young man, but now look—and he waved a cigar in the direction of his head. He said that his daughter was in the Royal Air Force. I understood what he was saying but was too shy to say anything myself.

That's all that was said about me. The conversation went back to the usual guns, howitzers and airplanes. I understood nearly everything, including the fact that the interpreter, V. N. Pavlov, was giving an accurate translation. But I wasn't allowed to listen long. My father kissed me and told me to go on about my own business. I couldn't understand why he had wanted to show me off to Churchill. But I think I see why now. He wanted to seem at least a little like an ordinary human being. You could see he liked Churchill.

I was in the tenth grade starting that October. Our teachers were of old, prewar vintage. Half the students had been evacuated and there were a good many new faces. The school was cold. But the classes of Anna Yasnopolskaya, the best teacher of literature in all Moscow, were warming to the mind and heart. We had a wide-ranging curriculum that winter. We started with Goethe and Schiller. Then we read Chekov and Gorky. We then moved on to poetry from the Acmeists[1] to Mayakovsky and Yesenin and the whole of Soviet literature.

At that time I lived in the world of art, the world of music, literature and painting, in which I was only just getting interested and which was also taught by Anna Yasnopolskaya. All of us took art very seriously and were drunk on poetry and heroic emotions. In his wonderful poem, "Fatal Years, the Forties," David Samoilov wrote:

> How these things all came together:
> War, disaster, dreams and youth. . . .
> How deeply it all impressed itself
> To awaken only later!

It was in that winter of 1942-43 that I met Alexei Yakovlevich Kapler. Because of him, my relationship with my father was ruined.

⇛ 16

Alexei Kapler is all right now and is living in Moscow. He's writing film scripts, giving seminars and teaching at the Institute of Cinematography. He is one of the older, recognized masters of film making. After ten years of exile and prison camps he's leading a normal life again, like so many people who've come through and weathered the blows of fate.

We saw each other only a few hours in all in the winter of 1942-43 and twelve years later, in 1955, again for a few fleeting hours. That's all there was to it: a brief encounter between a schoolgirl and a man of forty and a short sequel later on.

It was in late October, 1942, that Vasily brought Kapler to Zubalovo. Vasily was advising Kapler on a projected film about pilots in the air force. He also got to know Roman Karmen,[1] M. Slutsky, Konstantin Simonov[2] and Y. Voitekhov in this

173

connection, but the project itself never got beyond some noisy
drinking. At first, I guess, we made no special impression on
each other, Kapler and I. Later, however, we were all invited
to a film preview on Gnezdnikovsky Street, and he and I got to
talking for the first time. We talked about movies.

Kapler, or Lyusia as he was known, was surprised I knew
something about movies and pleased that I didn't like American hits with tap dancing and chorus girls. He suggested that
he'd like to show me some good films of his own choosing. The
next time he came to Zubalovo he showed us *Queen Christina*
with Greta Garbo. I was tremendously impressed, and that
pleased Kapler very much.

We next met during the November 7 holidays. A lot of people had come to the *dacha*. There was Simonov with Valya
Serova, Voitekhov and L. Tselikovskaya, and Karmen and his
wife, a well-known Moscow beauty named Nina. There were
some pilots and I can't remember who else besides. After a
rather boisterous dinner we started dancing. Kapler turned to
me unexpectedly: "Can you do the fox trot?" I was wearing
my first good dress from a dressmaker. I also had on an old
garnet brooch of my mother's and a pair of low-heeled shoes.
I was probably very awkward-looking, but Kapler assured me
that I was a good dancer. I was so much at ease and I felt so
peaceful and warm beside him! I had an extraordinary feeling
of trust in this big, agreeable man. I wanted to put my head on
his shoulder and quietly close my eyes.

"Why are you so unhappy today?" he asked me, never thinking what the answer might be. I kept on dancing, but I started
telling him everything. I told him how lonely I was at home
and how out of place I felt with my brother and relatives. I told
him it was ten years to the day since my mother's death, yet
nobody seemed to remember and there wasn't a soul I could
talk to about it. It all came pouring out, and the whole time we

went on dancing. They kept playing records and no one paid any attention to us.

That evening we reached out to each other. We were no longer strangers but friends. Kapler was surprised and moved. He had a talent for mixing in an easy, natural way with men and women of the greatest diversity. He was friendly, good-natured and interested in everything. But he, too, must have been lonely somehow. Maybe he was in need of someone. too.

He'd just come back from gathering material in an area where guerrilla warfare was being waged in Belorussia. He was living in an unheated hotel, the Savoy (now the Berlin), in Moscow, and his friends, war correspondents mostly, used to come to see him at the hotel.

We were irresistibly drawn to one another. Kapler had to stay in Moscow a few days after the holiday and then go to Stalingrad. During these few days we tried to see each other as much as we could, although it was unbelievably difficult with the life I had to lead. But Kapler used to come to my school and stand in the doorway of the building next door watching for me to come out. Knowing he was there, I could feel my heart tighten with joy. We used to go to the Tretyakov Gallery, now scarcely heated at all, and look at the exhibition on the war. We wandered there by the hour until all the closing bells rang because we had nowhere to go. We also went to the theater. Alexander Korneichuk's play *The Front* had just opened. Kapler said it had nothing to do with art. For some reason we also saw Maeterlinck's *The Blue Bird,* and we went to see *The Queen of Spades* at the Bolshoi. Kapler admitted that he couldn't stand opera, but we enjoyed strolling in the foyer.

Kapler showed me Disney's *Snow White and the Seven Dwarfs* and the wonderful *Young Mr. Lincoln* in the viewing room of the Ministry of Cinematography on Gnezdnikovsky Street. There we could sit side by side and alone.

Kapler also brought me books. He had gotten his hands on Hemingway's *For Whom the Bell Tolls** and gave it to me to read. He also brought Richard Aldington's *All Men Are Enemies* and Hemingway's *To Have and Have Not*. Then he gave me what are sometimes called "adult" books with a love interest, altogether confident that I would understand it all. I'm not sure I did at the time, but I remember those books as vividly as if I had read them yesterday.

Kapler presented me with his copy of the enormous *Anthology of Russian Poetry from Symbolism to the Present Day*. It was covered with marks and little crosses around his favorite poems. I've known the verses of Akhmatova,[3] Gumilov[4] and Khodasevich[5] by heart ever since. What a collection it was! I had it with me at home, and the number of times I've drawn comfort from it!

Together we walked the snowy streets of war-darkened Moscow, unable to get our fill of talking and of each other. My hapless "watchdog" Mikhail Klimov brought up the rear. He was utterly demoralized by what was happening, and particularly by the fact that Kapler never failed to greet him with the utmost amiability and give him a light for his cigarettes. We weren't inhibited by his presence, somehow. As for him, he looked on us with no ill will, at least for the time being.

To me Kapler was the cleverest, kindest, most wonderful person on earth. He radiated knowledge and all its fascination. He helped me discover the world of art, which was new to me and which I was only beginning to explore. As for me, I was a continual source of surprise to him. He found it extraordinary that I listened and understood and drank in all his words and that they found a response in me.

* This was in a Russian translation, which was already circulating privately. Yet it hasn't been published to this day!

Kapler soon left for Stalingrad. It was on the eve of the battle. He knew I would want to know everything he was seeing, and he took a step that was staggering in both its chivalry and recklessness. As I looked through *Pravda* one day in late November I came across an article entitled "Letters of Lieutenant L. from Stalingrad—Letter One," by Special Correspondent A. Kapler. It was a letter from a soldier to the woman he loved describing everything going on in Stalingrad—events the whole world was riveted on at that time.

The moment I saw it, I froze. I could just imagine my father's reaction when he opened the paper. The fact was, he had already been informed of my peculiar conduct. He had hinted to me once in a tone of extreme displeasure that I was behaving in a manner that could not be tolerated. I had ignored the hint and gone on behaving as before, but now he would undoubtedly see the article, which made the whole thing only too clear. Our walks in the Tretyakov were described in minute detail. He'd even had to end the article: "It's probably snowing now in Moscow. You can see the crenelated wall of the Kremlin from your window." What on earth would happen now?

Kapler got back from Stalingrad just before New Year's, 1943. As soon as we met I begged him not to see me or call me on the phone any more. I sensed that the whole thing might come to a terrible end. He was worried, too, and said he hadn't sent the article to *Pravda* but his "friends had played a trick on him." Apparently he, too, was aware that we were attracting dangerous attention, and he agreed we would have to part.

For two or three weeks, all the rest of January, we never even talked on the telephone. But we thought about each other all the more. Twelve years later we were able to compare notes about what had happened to us both. Kapler had lain on the sofa all those weeks. He refused to go out and just stared at the telephone.

I was the first to weaken. I called him on the telephone and the whole thing started up again. Every day we talked at least an hour on the phone. Everyone in my house was in a state of terror.

A decision was taken to bring Kapler to his senses somehow or other. Colonel Rumyantsev, General Vlasik's right hand and closest aide and another of my father's bodyguards, called Kapler on the telephone. They knew everything there was to know about us—and more. Rumyantsev suggested to Kapler in a diplomatic way that he should go as far away as possible on an assignment. Kapler told him he could go to hell and hung up.

The whole month of February we went to the movies and the theater or simply out walking. We sensed that the clouds hanging over us were growing darker. The last day of February was my seventeenth birthday. We longed to sit quietly together that day and couldn't think how to manage it. Neither of us could go to the other's home, so we had to find neutral territory. We hit upon an empty apartment near the Kursk Station where some air force friends of Vasily's used to forgather. I didn't go alone, but in the company of my "watchdog" Klimov. He was terrified when I set out after school that day in a wholly different direction than usual. He sat in an adjoining room the whole time pretending to read a paper while actually straining to catch what was going on in the next room, the door of which was wide open.

What was actually going on? We were neither of us capable of carrying on a conversation any longer. We stood together and kissed one another in silence, knowing it was the last time. Kapler knew it could only end badly and had decided to go away. He had been assigned to go to Tashkent to make a movie on the partisans in Belorussia called *In Defense of the Fatherland*. We were happy and grief-stricken at the same time. We gazed into each other's eyes and kissed. We were endlessly happy. But the tears kept coming into our eyes.

Alas, those who were watching had twisted everything in their own way, in line with the laws and yardsticks that governed their own behavior. And the reports they filed reflected their misinterpretation of the facts. And so on that day, my birthday, February 28, the decision on "what to do" with us had already been taken.

I went home crushed and tired, heavy with foreboding. My "watchdog" trailed along behind me, also trembling with apprehension over what might happen to him next.

Kapler went home to get his things, expecting to be leaving Moscow within a few days. Tatyana Tess came to see him the next day. Twelve years later, both of them described to me how he had sat there, sad and depressed.

The day after that, March 2, 1943, just as he was about to leave, two men appeared in his room and told him to come along. They took him straight to the Lubianka Prison. There Kapler saw our famous General Vlasik, who'd come to make sure everything went as it was supposed to. And everything did. Kapler was searched and told he was under arrest. The pretext was that he'd had contacts with foreigners. He had, in fact, been abroad several times and knew practically every foreign correspondent in Moscow. This was true, and he couldn't deny it. And it was all they had to have to accuse him of anything they liked. My name, of course, was never mentioned. And so Kapler embarked on a very different life, a life that went on for ten years.

I, of course, knew none of this at the time. This is what happened to me.

On the morning of March 3, as I was getting ready for school, my father showed up at the apartment unexpectedly, something he'd never done before. He strode briskly into my room. The look in his eyes alone was enough to rivet my nurse to the floor in one corner. I'd never seen my father look that way before. Generally restrained in his words and emotions, he was choking with anger and was nearly speechless. "Where, where are they all?" he spluttered. "Where are all these letters from your 'writer'?"

I can't describe the contempt in his voice as he spat out the word "writer." "I know the whole story! I've got all your telephone conversations right here!" He patted his pocket as he said it. "All right! Hand them over! Your Kapler is a British spy. He's under arrest!"

I took everything Kapler had ever written me out of my desk—his letters and the inscribed photographs he'd brought me from Stalingrad. There were notebooks of his, and sketches for short stories and a new movie script on Shostakovich. There was also a long farewell letter. He had given it to me on my birthday for me to remember him by.

"But I love him!" I protested at last, having found my tongue again.

"Love!" screamed my father, with a hatred of the very word I can scarcely convey. And for the first time in his life he slapped me across the face, twice. "Just look, nurse, how low she's sunk!" He could no longer restrain himself. "Such a war going on, and she's busy the whole time ———!" Unable to find any other expression, he used the coarse peasant word.

"No, no, no," was all my nurse could say, standing in her corner and warding off something frightful with her fat hand. "No, no, no!"

"What do you mean, no?" My father was still in a rage, but he was spent after hitting me and started speaking more calmly. "What do you mean, no, when I know the whole story!" He looked at me and said something that all but struck me down on the spot. "Take a look at yourself. Who'd want you? You fool! He's got women all around him!" With that he left. He went to the dining room and took all my letters, to read them with his own eyes.

I felt utterly broken. His last words had hit home. He could try to discredit Kapler in my eyes all he liked and he wouldn't get anywhere. But when he told me to "take a look at yourself," I realized right away no one could possibly want me. Could Kapler really have loved me after all? Could I really have meant anything to him?

I didn't get the point right away when my father flung out the words, "Your Kapler is a British spy." After he'd gone out the door I went on mechanically getting ready for school. It was only then that I realized what must have happened to Kapler. It was as though it were happening in a dream.

I was still in a daze when I got back from school that afternoon. I was told that "Your father wants to see you in the dining room." I went in silence. My father was tearing up Kapler's letters and photographs and throwing them into the wastebasket. "Writer!" he muttered. "He can't write decent Russian! She couldn't even find herself a Russian!" Apparently the fact that Kapler was a Jew was what bothered him most of all.

I was no longer capable of feeling anything. I didn't say a word and just went to my room. After that my father and I were estranged for a long time. We didn't speak to each other for months and didn't see one another till summer. Even then our relationship wasn't the same. I was never again the beloved daughter I had once been.

Kapler was sent to the north for five years. He lived in Vorkuta[6] and was allowed to work in the theater. After finishing his sentence, he decided to go to Kiev, where his parents were, since he was forbidden to go back to Moscow. In spite of the enormous risk, however, he came to Moscow for a very brief stay. The year was 1948.

After a few days in Moscow, he boarded the train for Kiev. Some plain-clothes men came after him and took him off at the next station. Once again, he was dispatched in quite a different direction from the one he'd set out for. This time he wasn't sent to a town like Vorkuta, but to a prison camp instead. He was sentenced to work in the mines in the terrible camps near Inta.[7] He'd been given a five-year sentence for disobeying the ban on visiting Moscow. For five years he worked in a mine.

In March, 1953, when his term was coming to an end, he asked for permission to return to Vorkuta, where he'd worked in the theater and hoped to settle. Instead, he was unexpectedly taken again to the Lubianka in Moscow.

He was released shortly afterward, in July of 1953. This time he was told: "You are free now. You can go home. What's your address? Whom do you want to telephone?"

And so he walked out of prison and onto the streets of Moscow, which he hadn't seen in so many years, onto the scorching July streets and boulevards.

For ten whole years I'd heard almost nothing reliable about Kapler. The life I led was such that I couldn't see his friends without its being known. I knew only that he'd been sent to the north for "contacts with foreigners." I didn't even know he'd been in Moscow for a short time in 1948.

I had nothing but a memory of the moments of happiness Kapler had given me.

Then came March 3, 1953. It was ten years to the day since my father had come into my room in a rage and struck me across the face. Now I was sitting by his bed as he lay dying. I was watching the doctors bustling around, but my thoughts occasionally wandered. I thought about Kapler. It was exactly ten years since his arrest. What had happened to him? What was he doing now?

A year later, at the Second Congress of Soviet Writers in the Kremlin, I ran into Kapler in the glitter of St. George's Hall. It was eleven years since we had seen one another.

→» *17*

I graduated from school in the spring of 1941. After that third of March my father and I didn't meet or even talk on the telephone for four months. Finally I phoned him in July to tell him I'd graduated from school. "Come out here!" he growled. I showed him my diploma and told him I wanted to enter the university and take up literary studies. Encouraged by my teacher Anna Yasnopolskaya, I wanted to follow my interest in literature.

"It's one of those literary types you want to be!" muttered my father in a tone of displeasure. "You want to be one of those Bohemians! They're uneducated, the whole lot, and you want to be just like them. No, you'd better get a decent education—let it be history. Writers need social history, too. Study history. Then you can do what you want."

184

That was his summary of the situation. Dogmatic though it was, and although one of my friends and I were already studying for our entrance examinations in literature, I once again trusted in my father's authority and went into history.

I've never regretted it. History has indeed proved useful. But what my father failed to foresee was that I didn't turn out to be the "educated Marxist" he'd hoped for. Precisely because of my study of social history at the university it worked out quite differently.

Once again it was boring and quiet at home. Zubalovo was closed in the spring of 1943 because, as my father remarked, we'd turned it into a den of iniquity. When my grandparents got back from the south that summer, they went into a rest home called "The Pines."

Yakov's little girl Gulia was reunited with her mother, who had spent two years in prison under the statute providing for punishment of relatives of those who have been taken prisoner. (Everyone who was taken prisoner, even if they'd been wounded, as Yakov was, was considered to have "surrendered voluntarily to the enemy." The government thereby washed its hands of millions of its own officers and men during the war and refused to have anything to do with them. Is it any wonder that when the war ended many of them didn't want to come home?)

Vasily was banished from Zubalovo, as I was, for "moral depravity." In addition, he was given ten days in a punishment cell by personal order of my father in his capacity as Minister of Defense.[1]

Things were topsy-turvy at the apartment, too. To my great joy, Alexandra Nakashidze was fired. All her spying on me, her burrowing into my letters and notebooks and her eavesdropping on my telephone conversations with Kapler, all of it put together hadn't been enough to save her. My father was fed up with her stupidity. Besides, she hadn't done her job. She had failed to protect me from temptation. She soon married a rather highly placed Georgian and left us for good. She was glad of it herself.

My "watchdog" Mikhail Klimov was also taken off the job in the autumn of 1943, when I started at the university. I begged my father to abolish this kind of protection because it made me feel ashamed in front of the rest of the students. To my surprise, my father understood and agreed.

My nurse was the only one left, and she stayed with me until her death in 1956. She went on sewing in her room next to mine, just as she always had, and I could hear the whirr of her sewing machine. She'd slip in quietly and put a plate of pared apples in front of me, or some tea with little slices of bread and butter. And I'd sit there buried in my books.

I now saw my father only once in a great while. He stopped coming for dinner, as he used to, and started going back to Kuntsevo for dinner every night accompanied by the usual entourage. The war was coming to an end. The turning point had been reached.

In the spring of 1944 I got married. My first husband, Grigory Morozov, was a student at the Institute of International Relations. I had known him from our school days together. He was Jewish, and my father didn't like it. However, not wanting to go too far again, he somehow accepted the marriage and gave his consent.

I went out one day to see him about it especially. We didn't say much, as it was hard for me by this time to carry on a conversation with him at all. I had let him down, and he was displeased with me once and for all.

It was May. Flowers were in bloom outside the *dacha*. The bird-cherry trees were a dazzling white, bees were buzzing, and it was still. "So you want to get married, do you?" he remarked. For a long time he stared at the trees and said nothing. "Yes, it's spring," he remarked all of a sudden. "To hell with you. Do as you like."

It was a meaningful phrase, for it meant he wouldn't put any obstacle in the way. And he was as good as his word. For the next three years we were well provided for. We went on with our studies in peace. I was able to have a child and not have to worry about it. For a long time the baby was looked after not by one nurse but by two: mine and the nurse who'd brought up my niece Gulia, Yakov's little girl. It meant we were being given all a good parent could provide.

We were given an apartment outside the Kremlin. My father set only one condition on the marriage: that my husband never set foot in his house. We were even rather glad. There was just one thing he wouldn't give us: his love, warmth, a real family relationship. He never once met my first husband and said quite firmly that he never would.

"He's too calculating, that young man of yours," he told me. "Just think. It's terrible at the front. People are getting shot. And look at him. He's sitting it out at home."

I kept quiet and didn't insist that they meet. It would have turned out badly in any case.

I saw my father very rarely. After our meeting in the spring it was half a year, autumn, before we saw one another again. I told him I was going to have a child. He softened and allowed us to go out to Zubalovo again. "You need country air," he said.

We started going there again, just the two of us. How empty it was! Vasily was at the front with his division, and later his corps. He rose higher and higher. He became a general. He was awarded orders and medals. And he was drinking more and more.

Early on the morning of May 9, when the radio announced

that the war was over, I telephoned my father. I was tremendously excited. Moscow was in an uproar. Early as it was, everyone knew it was Victory Day. "Congratulations on our victory,
Papa!" Barely able to speak, I wanted to weep for joy.

"Yes, we've won," he replied. "Thank you. And congratulations to you, too! How are you feeling?" Like everybody else
in Moscow that day, I was feeling fine!

My husband and I invited everyone we knew to our apartment. The place was jammed. Everyone was dancing, singing
and drinking champagne. The streets were packed. I was afraid
to go out, as I was expecting my child in two weeks. Indeed,
it was an easy birth. Everyone was so joyous and happy that
May of 1945!

I didn't see my father until August, when he got back from
the Potsdam Conference. The day I was out at his *dacha* he
had the usual visitors. They told him that the Americans had
dropped the first atom bomb over Japan. Everyone was busy
with that, and my father paid hardly any attention to me.

And I had such important news—to me, anyway! I had a son.
He was already three months old. His name was Josef.* But
this was such a little thing compared to the great events going
on around us. In a word, nobody cared. Besides, my brother
had said something uncomplimentary to my father about my
husband, and my father was cold, indifferent and withdrawn
as a result.

It was some time before we saw each other after that. My
father fell ill, and was quite sick for months. The tension and
fatigue of the war years and of his age were beginning to tell.
He was sixty-six by this time.

I don't remember seeing him in the winter of 1945-46,
though possibly I did. I was back at the university making up

* My first father-in-law's name was also Josef. The boy was named after both
grandfathers.

the year I'd lost on account of the baby. My husband and I were living in our apartment in Moscow and were both at the university. Our baby, Josef, was at Zubalovo with both nurses, his and mine. Apparently my father thought that since I had everything I needed there was nothing I could possibly want from him. His mind was made up that he would never on any condition meet my husband.

My father never asked me to divorce him. He never expressed a desire for me to do any such thing. We broke up after three years, in the spring of 1947, for reasons of a personal nature. I was therefore very much surprised later on to hear it rumored that my father had insisted on a divorce.

By that time I'd probably seen my father twice more. He went south in the summer of 1946 on his first vacation since 1937. He traveled by car. The whole procession stretched out a long way over roads that were still very bad in those days. (They started building a highway to Simferopol, in the Crimea, shortly afterward.) The procession stopped in towns along the way. They all stayed overnight with the Secretaries of the district and province committees of the Communist Party. My father wanted to see for himself how people were living. What he saw was havoc wrought by the war on every side.

The housekeeper Valechka, who accompanied my father on all his journeys, told me recently how upset he was when he saw that people were still living in dugouts and that everything was still in ruins. She also told me how some Party leaders who later rose very high came to see him in the south and report on agricultural conditions in the Ukraine. They brought watermelons and other melons so huge you couldn't put your arms around them. They brought fruit and vegetables and golden sheaves of grain, the point being to show off how rich the Ukraine was. Meanwhile the chauffeur of one leader, whose name happened to be Nikita Khrushchev, told the servants there was a famine in the Ukraine, that there was nothing to eat in the countryside and peasant women were using their cows for plowing.

"It's a wonder they weren't ashamed," wailed Valechka, the tears streaming down her face. "To deceive your father of all people! And now they're blaming him for it, too!"

After this journey they started building more vacation houses in the south. They were now called "government *dachas.*" The idea was that they were for the use of all the members of the Politburo, but in fact the only ones who used them were Molotov, Zhdanov[2] and my father. A *dacha* was built at Novy Afon, another not far from Sukhumi, and a whole cluster were built on Lake Ritsa. Another *dacha* was built in the Valdai Hills in Novgorod Province in the north.

My father was pleased, of course, when I was divorced from my first husband, whom he never approved of. His attitude toward me softened after that, but not for long. I was a source of irritation to him and hadn't turned out the way he hoped at all. But he was affectionate with my son.

He invited me to Kholodnaya Rechka, in Sochi, in August, 1947. We were there for three weeks. It was the first time we'd been together in years. It was pleasant and sad and tremendously taxing, all at once. As usual, I couldn't make the adjustment to his mixed-up schedule of sleeping half the day, having a meal at three in the afternoon and dinner at ten in the evening, and then sitting up half the night at the dinner table with his colleagues.

He was difficult to talk to. Strange as it may seem, we had nothing to say to one another. When we were alone, I'd rack my brain trying to think of something to talk about. I always felt as though I were standing at the foot of a high mountain.

He was up above and I was shouting to him, straining with every ounce of energy I possessed to reach him, but an isolated word here or there was all that was getting through. Only scattered words of his got through to me, too, and you can't have much of a conversation that way. It was easier when we went walking. And he enjoyed having me read him his newspapers and magazines aloud. He had aged. He wanted peace and quiet. Rather, he didn't know himself just what it was he wanted. In the evening we looked at old, prewar movies, like *Volga-Volga*, which he liked very much, and films by Chaplin.

The whole crowd would come for dinner: Beria, Malenkov, Zhdanov, Bulganin and the rest. I found it dull and exhausting to sit three or four hours at the table listening to the same old stories as if there were no news and nothing whatever going on in the world! It made me dead tired and I would go off to bed. They sat up late into the night.*

I soon went back to Moscow and the university. I was again living in our deserted apartment in the Kremlin. It was like a tomb. Vasily had his own apartment in town. Even Alexandra Nakashidze's duties as a housekeeper had been taken over by a commandant, a captain or major of State Security named Ivan Borodachev, who treated the treasures entrusted to him as if they were sacred and even entered in his notebook the names of the books I carried out of my father's library and into the dining room to read. I had my son and nurse with me, and my nurse pared apples and brought them to me on a plate while I was studying, just as she always had before.

I had a letter from my father that fall, the first in a long, long time. It was a far-off echo of prewar days, far off and somehow quite different.

* Milovan Djilas has given a good description of evenings of this kind in his book *Conversations with Stalin*.

HELLO, SVETKA!

I got your letter. It's good you haven't forgotten your father. I'm well. Everything's fine. I'm not lonely. I'm sending you some little presents—tangerines. I send you a kiss.

YOUR J. STALIN

October 11, 1947

These years, 1947 to 1949, were a very dreary time. My life was frightfully isolated. It was a long time since I'd had Mikhail Klimov following at my heels, but still I was under surveillance every step I took. Little Josef was growing up a child of nature at Zubalovo, and I sometimes didn't see him for weeks at a time. I trudged back and forth between home and the university. I went to the Conservatory often but seldom to the theater. I didn't know many people and found it impossible to get to know anybody new.

I frequently went to the Zhdanovs' house, especially after Andrei Zhdanov's death. Compared with my own dismal fortress, the Zhdanovs' house seemed very cheerful. Every Sunday Yury Zhdanov's friends from school and the university used to come there, people whom both of us knew. It was an oasis in my solitary, almost wasteland existence. I enjoyed going there. All the other young people seemed to be so much at ease. My father had been very fond of Andrei Zhdanov. He respected the son and had always hoped the two families might one day be linked in marriage. It happened in the spring of 1949 as a matter of hard common sense but without any special love or affection. I thought I would gain at least a little freedom by moving to his house and that it would give me the access to people that I lacked.

But my father may have had other ideas. I suddenly learned he was having a second floor added to the *dacha* at Kuntsevo. He showed up one day at Zubalovo. Roaming from room to room, he inquired, "What do you want to move to the

Zhdanovs' for? You'll be eaten alive by the women there," he went on. "There are too many women in that house!" The question of marriage was already settled, but I wanted to finish at the university first and move to the Zhdanovs' then. My father knew everyone in the Zhdanov household and couldn't stand either the widow or the sisters. I was alarmed, because I had no desire whatsoever to live in my father's house and knew that Yury Andreyevich would never agree for anything on earth.

As he'd gotten older my father had begun feeling lonely. He was so isolated from everyone by this time, so elevated, that he seemed to be living in a vacuum. He hadn't a soul he could talk to.

In 1948 he sent me to the Crimea with my son Josef and with Yakov's little girl Gulia, whom he once in a while thought to ask about. I had a letter from him while I was there: "Come by the tenth and we'll go south together. I send you a kiss. Your little papa." He wanted us all to go together to Kholodnaya Rechka, as we had the year before. But I decided against it. I wanted to spend August at Zubalovo with my nurse and son, and that offended him.

I went south to see him later, in November of 1948. It was warm and sunny. Cold as the sea felt, it was caressing to the eye. The roses were in bloom and you could go out without a coat. My father was angry at me. He summoned me to the table and bawled me out and called me a "parasite" in front of everyone. He told me "no good had come" of me yet. Everyone was silent and embarrassed. I didn't know what to say and was silent, too.

The next day he suddenly started talking to me for the first time about my mother and the way she died. We were by ourselves. The anniversary of her death, November 8, fell during the November 7 holiday every year. It ruined the holiday for him for all time, and in his last years he tried to spend November in the south.

I was at a loss. I had no idea what to say—I was afraid of the subject. We were sitting over a long lunch, alone. As always, there was good wine and plenty of fruit. "What a miserable little pistol it was," he remarked, suddenly angry and showing me with his fingers just how small it was. "It was nothing but a toy. Pavlusha brought it to her. A fine thing to give anybody!"

He cast about for other culprits. He wanted to find the reason and someone to whom he could shift the burden of blame. It weighed on him more and more. Apparently as he got older he started thinking of my mother with increasing frequency. Suddenly he remembered Polina Zhemchuzhina, Molotov's wife, and how close she'd been to my mother, and decided that she'd "had a bad influence on her." Then he started cursing *The Green Hat,* the book my mother had been reading not long before she died. He didn't want to dwell on other more important reasons, on the things that had made their life together so hard for her. He was looking for some simple, direct cause, as though that was all there was to it. It was painful and difficult for me. For the first time I felt he was talking about it with me as an adult and an equal and as though he had complete—well, not quite complete—trust in me. But I'd rather have fallen through the ground than have had that kind of trust.

We returned to Moscow together on the train that November of 1948. I was sitting in my compartment glancing at photographs of paintings in the magazine *Art* when my father came in and took a look. "What's that?" he asked. It was drawings and sketches by the painter Repin. "And I've never even seen them," he remarked suddenly, with such sadness in his voice that it made me feel very badly.

For a moment I tried to imagine what would happen if my father suddenly descended on the Tretyakov Gallery, or rather went there on a special day when it was closed to the public and open only to him personally. Lord, what a fuss there'd be over that! What a lot of nonsense and running around. And how much rehashing later! Probably my father himself was aware that it just wasn't open to him, like so many of the pastimes other people were able to enjoy. And so he let it alone. Maybe he was afraid. I don't know. But he wasn't afraid of people, ever, and the hypocritical remarks you hear today to the effect that "He didn't like the people" sound absurd to me.

As we pulled in at the various stations, we'd go for a stroll along the platform. My father would walk as far as the engine, giving greetings to the railway workers as he went. You couldn't see a single passenger. It was a special train, and no one was allowed on the platform. It was a sinister, sad, depressing sight. Who ever thought up such a thing? Who had contrived all these stratagems? Not he. It was the system of which he himself was a prisoner and in which he was stifling from loneliness, emptiness and lack of human companionship.

By the time we reached Moscow I was acutely distressed. The train stopped before it got to the station, outside Moscow somewhere, and our automobiles were driven up to it. Again, they were avoiding the city because of all the people there. General Vlasik, puffed up and fat from cognac and self-importance, was fussing and running back and forth. The generals and colonels of the bodyguard, every one of whom had grown fat at state expense, were also puffing and blowing. A whole procession was on hand—court, retinue and hangers-on. My father ground his teeth when he saw them and never let an opportunity go by to insult them and shout crude words in their direction. He never spoke to his household servants in that tone of voice.

I went home to the Kremlin apartment, and he went to Kuntsevo. It took me several days before I felt like myself again. It was hard being with him. It cost me an enormous amount of nervous energy. We were very far apart, and both of us knew it. Each of us yearned to be back in his own home alone, to get a rest from the other. Each was ruffled and upset by the other. Each of us suffered and was sad. Why must life be so absurd? And each of us thought the other was to blame.

A new wave of arrests got under way at the end of 1948. My two aunts, the widows of Uncle Pavel and Redens, were sent to prison, and so was everyone who knew them. J. G. Morozov, the father of my first husband, was arrested, too. Next there was a campaign against people who were called "cosmopolitan," and a whole new group of people were arrested. They even arrested Molotov's wife, undaunted by the thought of the terrible blow they were inflicting on Molotov himself. Lozovsky was arrested, and Mikhoels[3] was killed. All of them were lumped together in a single alleged "Zionist center."

"That first husband of yours was thrown your way by the Zionists," my father told me a little later on. "Papa," I tried to object, "the younger ones couldn't care less about Zionism." "No! You don't understand," was the sharp answer. "The entire older generation is contaminated with Zionism, and now they're teaching the young people, too." It was no use arguing with him.

When I asked him, he told me what my aunts were guilty of. "They talked a lot. They knew too much and they talked too much. And it helped our enemies." He was bitter, as bitter as he could be against the whole world.

He saw enemies everywhere. It had reached the point of

being pathological, of persecution mania, and it was all a result of being lonely and desolate.

"You yourself make anti-Soviet statements," he told me one day angrily and in complete earnest. I didn't try to object or ask where he got that from.

I wanted to get away from home—it hardly mattered where. I took my final examinations in the spring of 1949 and married Yury Andreyevich Zhdanov. Little Josef and I went to the Zhdanovs' apartment in the Kremlin to live.

My father hadn't been far wrong. It was by no means as easy and pleasant at the Zhdanovs' as I'd thought. Our house was dreary, empty, quiet and uncomfortable. It wasn't easy living there, but one thing we never had, and that was cheapness of spirit.

Now, however, I found myself in a household where a show, albeit a purely external, hypocritical show, was made of what was called "Party spirit" on the one hand, while on the other hand there existed a dyed-in-the-wool acquisitiveness of the worst female kind. There were trunkloads of possessions. The whole setting, with its vases, antimacassars, and worthless still lifes on the walls, was vulgar and totally lacking in taste. The place was presided over by Zinaida Zhdanov, the widow and the ultimate embodiment of this mixture of Party bigotry and the complacency of the bourgeois woman. After we were married my husband's friends started coming less and less often, our circle narrowed down to the family, and it became hopelessly and intolerably dull.

The years 1949 to 1952 were terribly trying for me, as they were for everyone. The whole country was gasping for air. Things were unbearable for everyone. The most orthodox Party spirit reigned in the house I lived in, but it had nothing in common with the spirit of my grandfather and my grand-

mother, my mother, the Svanidzes and all the old Party people
I knew. It was all hypocritical, a caricature purely for show.

Even my husband Yury, who had graduated from the university and had always been one of the most popular people
there, was suffering on account of his work in the Central Committee. He didn't know, he couldn't imagine, what he'd gotten
himself into.[4] He wasn't home much. He came home late at
night, it being the custom in those years to work till eleven at
night. He had worries of his own and with his inborn lack of
emotion wasn't in the habit of paying much attention to my
woes or state of mind. When he was at home, moreover, he was
completely under his mother's thumb. He called her a "wise
old owl" and let himself be guided by her ways, her tastes and
her opinions.

I with my more easygoing upbringing very soon found it
impossible to breathe. I asked to have my old nurse come to
live with us there. She was the one person who was near and
dear to me. But they told me that "there would be absolutely
nothing for an ignorant old woman of her sort to do here. She
would only spoil Josef." And so my nurse stayed on at Zubalovo in a tiny room in the servants' quarters.

We'd drink tea and jam when I went out to see her. She told
me about her ailments and we'd talk about our affairs. She
came to see me at Uspenskoye, the Zhdanovs' country house,
two or three times, but they treated her with utmost conde-
scension—all except little Josef, who always flung himself on
"Granny," as he called her—and she would leave quickly. She
wasn't used to being treated that way. All her life, no matter
whom she worked for, she'd been treated as one of the family.
Even the families of the nobility she had worked for before the
Revolution treated her better than the Zhdanovs. It hurt her
pride.

I didn't see my father for a long, long time. During the winter of 1949-50 I was quite ill. I was expecting a child and, unlike the first time, was having a lot of trouble. I went to the hospital in the spring. I finally returned to Uspenskoye in the summer, a month and a half later, with my tiny, weak little Katya. I was worn out from being lonely and sick, from the realization that my second marriage was a failure and from distaste for the house I had to live in.

It happened that Svetlana Molotov, whom I'd known from childhood, was in the next bed in the hospital. She had also given birth to a little girl. Two days later her father came to see her just like any other father. Because of my long illness, my nerves were at the breaking point, and the comparison made me sorry for myself. That night I wrote my father a woe-begone letter telling him how miserable I was. I received a reply two days later and was glad to have any answer at all. It was the last letter I was ever to receive from him.

DEAR SVETOCHKA!

I got your letter. I'm very glad you got off so lightly. Kidney trouble is a serious business. To say nothing of having a child. Where did you ever get the idea that I had abandoned you?! It's the sort of thing people dream up. I advise you not to believe your dreams. Take care of yourself. Take care of your daughter, too. The state needs people, even those who are born prematurely. Be patient a little longer—we'll see each other soon. I kiss my Svetochka.

YOUR LITTLE PAPA

May 10, 1950

I was pleased with the letter. I was glad to have an answer because I hadn't especially counted on getting one. But it made me terribly uneasy to think that the state already needed my little Katya, whose life was still in the balance. And I was fairly certain that he and I wouldn't see each other so "soon."

It wasn't until more than a year later, in the summer of

1951, that my father and I actually spent some time together again. He summoned me to Borzhomi, Georgia, to be with him on his vacation, and I went for two weeks. He was having a rest, and I could see he was enjoying the sweet-smelling Georgian air and the fresh breeze off the Kura River that flowed alongside the Likani Palace in which he was staying. I realized that something had drawn him there all of a sudden. He was seventy-two by this time, but his stride was brisk as he walked through the park with the fat generals of the bodyguard panting to keep up with him. Suddenly he would change course and run right into them. It made him explode with anger, and he scolded the first one who happened to be handy on some trivial pretext or other.

As always in summer, he had lunch and dinner under a tree in the garden. He asked the servants to catch him some fresh fish in the Kura. He could remember from his childhood the Georgian names for the various fish and was pleased at the memories they brought to mind. But he never said so in so many words. He didn't like talking about his feelings and used to remark that that kind of thing was "for women."

The one thing he did mention was that he had stayed in the Likani Palace with my mother in 1922 when they came to Georgia after Vasily was born. He didn't go into the details.

The "palace" was an old hunting lodge that had once belonged to some prince or other. It was poorly constructed and lacking in taste, but it was in a lovely setting in a gorge of the Kura River. One of the banks was steep and piled with rocks out of which jutted the ruins of an old castle, a common sight in Georgia. The other bank had a gentle slope to it. A combination forest and park had been laid out and planted in a small mountain valley, and that's where the hunting lodge was. The service quarters were so cramped that the house was anything but comfortable for the enormous retinue that accompanied my father everywhere he went. The generals and commandants could curse all they liked, but as usual my father was enjoying having a whole house to himself.

My father had unpleasant memories of his journey here because he couldn't stand the sight of a crowd applauding him and shouting "Hurrah!" His face would twitch with annoyance each time it happened. Here, at the Kutaisi railway station, his Georgian countrymen had given him such a reception that he'd been unable to leave the train and get into his car. People literally threw themselves under the wheels. They crawled and shouted and threw flowers and carried their children on their shoulders. Here if nowhere else, it was warm-blooded, unfeigned and sincere. Here if anywhere it was straight from the heart, but my father was angry anyway. He was accustomed by this time to having the stations empty and cleared for his arrival and to the roads he traveled on being empty. He wasn't used to people shouting and hurling themselves at his car. He had altogether forgotten that feelings of this kind could be sincere and not put on.

After that he made one attempt to go from Borzhomi to Bakuriani, but when he was halfway there he turned back. At the first village he came to there were carpets over the road. The villagers swarmed onto the road and stopped the car. My father had to get out and join them at the banquet table. Thank heaven I wasn't with him. I'd have been overwhelmed by embarrassment.

I was horribly embarrassed even by the more modest "homage" paid us when we went to the Bolshoi Theater in Moscow and at the banquets in honor of my father's seventieth birthday. I was always afraid my father might at any moment say something that would throw cold water on everyone, and also I could see his face twitching with annoyance. "They open their mouths and yell like fools," he would say in a tone of

angry contempt. Did he perceive the hypocrisy that lay behind "homage" of this sort? I think so, for he was astonishingly
sensitive to hypocrisy and was impossible to lie to. Possibly
he was so desolate and empty inside by this time that he no
longer believed people were capable of being genuinely
warmhearted and sincere, even in Georgia, where the simple
peasants couldn't really be suspected of putting on a show of
rejoicing.

Apparently the Georgians decided to show everyone they
were independent of the secret police in Moscow and all its discipline and prove that in Georgia people were free to express
their feelings any way they liked. As a result my father couldn't
go to Tbilisi or Gori, much as he may have wanted to. He
simply sat in Borzhomi, a prisoner of his own fame, and didn't
dare stir off the land surrounding the hunting lodge.

It was late autumn before he returned that year, and I
went back to Moscow ahead of him. When we left Borzhomi,
Vasily and I stopped off at my father's birthplace in Gori.
Suddenly I felt as if I'd been born here, too.

Gori is in a little valley in a bend of the Kura, which winds
around a flat hill topped by a fortress. At the foot of the hill
is a village. Everywhere there are orchards, sunlight and vineyards, and the silver Kura, shallow and quiet-flowing. The
surrounding mountains drop into a ravine and the village of
Ateni. The place boasts a wonderful golden wine and a church
with classic Georgian architecture and eleventh-century fres-
coes.

My heart turned over when I first saw this church set
among vineyards and the village among orchards of peaches
and pears. It's like a bowl of abundant soil with a dome of
blue sky and more sunshine than any other place on earth.
Unfortunately our visit was marred by official homage and an
inspection of the so-called Stalin house and museum. The

house is nothing but a poor cobbler's hut. But Beria had a marble pavilion built over it that makes the place look like one of the lesser subway stations in Moscow. Under the marble canopy you can barely see the little hovel, which ought to have been left as it was and could perfectly well have told its story without the marble. Everything was treated like a relic. The people showing us around were trembling with reverence. I was in an agony of embarrassment, and my only thought was to get out of there as fast as possible.

I thought about my Grandmother Yekaterina while I was in Georgia that fall. She's buried near the writer Griboyedov on St. David's Hill in Tbilisi, close by St. David's Church. The place has a quiet beauty that hasn't been cheapened or spoiled.

I thought back to the time when Yakov, Vasily and I were sent to call on my grandmother in Tbilisi in 1934, when she was ill. Maybe Beria was the instigator of the visit, because it was at his house that we stayed. We spent about a week in his magnificent apartment in Tbilisi and his equally sumptuous *dacha* outside the city, and only about half an hour with my grandmother.

She lived in a beautiful old palace with a park. Her room was small and dark, with a low ceiling and little windows facing on a courtyard. There were an iron cot and a screen in one corner. The room was full of old women wearing black, as old women do in Georgia, and a little old lady was perched on the narrow iron cot. We were led up to her. She gave each of us an awkward embrace with hands that were knotted and bony. She kissed us and spoke a few words in Georgian. Yakov was the only one who understood. He answered while we stood quietly by.

I remember that she had light eyes and that her hands and her pale face were covered with freckles. She was wearing

a kerchief, but I knew Grandmother used to have red hair—
my father had told me so. Georgians, by the way, consider
red hair a sign of beauty. All the old women in the room were
friends of hers. They took turns kissing us, and they all said
I looked very much like my grandmother. She offered us hard
candies on a plate. The tears were rolling down her cheeks.

We couldn't spend much time with her because we literally
spoke different languages.

There was one sight I remember vividly. Beria's wife Nina
had come with us. She was seated next to Grandmother and
spent the whole time talking to her about something or other.
Yet I'm sure they despised each other. The room was full of
people gawking. There were bunches of herbs on the window
sills and the place smelled of them. We left quickly and didn't
pay any more visits to the "palace." Though I was only about
eight at the time, I wondered why Grandmother seemed so
poor. I'd never seen such an awful-looking black cot, though
I must say we didn't live in any great luxury at home then
either—just in reasonable comfort.

My grandmother had principles of her own. They were the
principles of one who was old and God-fearing, who'd lived
a life that was upright and hard, full of dignity and honor.
Changing her life in any way whatever was the furthest thing
from her mind. She passed on all her stubbornness and firm-
ness, her puritanical standards, her unbending, masculine
character and her high requirements for herself, to my father.
He was much more like her than like his father.

On my last visit I went to the place where she lies buried.
How could I have stood by her grave, so peaceful and still,
thinking about her life, without my thoughts turning to God,
in whom she believed so devoutly?

⇶ *18*

Nowadays when I read or hear somewhere that my father used to consider himself practically a god, it amazes me that people who knew him well can say such a thing.

It's true my father wasn't especially democratic, but he never thought of himself as a god.

His life was most solitary of all toward the end, his trip south in the autumn of 1951 being the last he ever took anywhere. He never left Moscow again and stayed at Kuntsevo practically all the time. Kuntsevo, meanwhile, was rebuilt over and over again. In his later years a little wooden house was built near the main house, as the air was fresher there. Often he spent days at a time in the big room with the fireplace. Since he didn't care for luxury, there was nothing luxurious about the room except the wood paneling and the valuable rug on the floor.

As for the presents which were sent to him from all corners of the earth,[1] he had them collected in one spot and donated them to a museum. It wasn't hypocrisy or a pose on his part, as a lot of people say, but simply the fact that he had no idea what to do with this avalanche of objects that were valuable, sometimes priceless: paintings, china, furniture, weapons, clothing, utensils and products of local craftsmanship from everywhere in the world.

Once in a while he gave one of them, a Rumanian or Bulgarian folk costume or something like that, to me. On the whole, however, he considered it wrong that any personal use should be made even of the things that were sent to me. Maybe he realized that the feelings that went into them were symbolic, and he thought the things themselves deserved to be treated as symbols.

In 1950 a Museum of Gifts was opened in Moscow. While my father was still alive and even after, women of my acquaintance used to tell me, "What a wonderful set of furniture!" Or: "What a marvelous record player! Couldn't they let you keep it?" But there could be no question of that.

I only saw my father twice after that last trip to Georgia. I've already told you how I took my children to his *dacha* in the autumn of 1952 for the November 7 anniversary. I also went there for his seventy-third birthday on December 21 of that year. It was the last time I saw him before I was called to his deathbed.

I was worried at how badly he looked.* He must have felt his illness coming on. Maybe he was aware of some hypertension, for he'd suddenly given up smoking and was very pleased with himself. It must have taken a lot of will power,

---

* After the Nineteenth Party Congress in October, 1952, he twice informed the Central Committee that he wished to retire. It was probably because he was ill. In any case the fact that he wanted to retire is known to everyone who belonged to the Central Committee at that time.

because he'd smoked for fifty or sixty years. He was probably aware of an increase in his blood pressure, but he hadn't any doctor to take care of him. Vinogradov, the only one he trusted, had been arrested and he wouldn't let any other doctor near him.

Somewhere or other he got hold of some quack remedies, and he'd take some pills or pour a few drops of iodine into a glass of water. Moreover, he himself did a thing no doctor would ever have allowed: Two months after I last saw him and just twenty-four hours before his stroke he went to the bath-house near the *dacha* and took a steam bath, as he'd been accustomed to doing ever since Siberia. There's no doctor on earth who'd have permitted such a thing, but he didn't have a doctor.

The "case of the Kremlin doctors" was under way that last winter. My father's housekeeper told me not long ago that my father was exceedingly distressed at the turn events took. She heard it discussed at the dinner table. She was waiting on the table, as usual, when my father remarked that he didn't believe the doctors were "dishonest" and that the only evidence against them, after all, was the "reports" of Dr. Timashuk.[2] Everyone, as usual, remained silent.

My father's housekeeper Valechka is biased. She doesn't want the least little shadow to fall on my father's name. But one has to listen to what she says, all the same, and extract any kernel of truth her stories may contain, since she was at least in the same house with him for the last eighteen years, while I was far away.

A lot of people were critical of me for not going to see him more often. "Why don't you go and see your father?" they'd ask. "Call him up and tell him you want to see him. And if he says no, call him again. Sooner or later he'll find the time."

Maybe they were right. Maybe I was too easily put off. But

he would often answer, "I'm busy," in a voice of anger and
irritation and slam the receiver down. It would take me a
long time after that to summon up strength to call him again.
Months might go by before I could bring myself to do it.

I'll tell you about the last time I was there, though naturally
I didn't realize it was the last time. We sat at the table as
usual and the usual people were present.* There was the usual
talk, the usual sharp asides, the same old jokes I'd been hearing for years.

In addition to the fact that my father wasn't smoking that
day, his face had a ruddy look in contrast to its usual pale-
ness. His blood pressure must have been terribly high already.
But he was taking little sips of light Georgian wine just as he
always did. Everything in the room seemed strange to me—
those awful portraits of writers on the walls, the "Reply of the
Zaporozhe Cossacks" painting, those children's photographs
taken from magazines. Another thing that seemed odd was the
fact that a man who wanted something to put on the walls
should never have considered hanging even one of the thousands of pictures he'd been given. True, there was a Chinese
needlepoint of an enormous, bright-colored tiger framed and
hanging in one corner, but it had been there since before the
war.

Everything was the same as ever at the table—not a single
new word. It was as though the outside world didn't even
exist. Could it really be that all these people sitting here
hadn't gleaned a single fresh or interesting piece of information from anywhere in the world that day? These people had

* Toward the end the "usual" people were Beria, Malenkov, Bulganin and
Mikoyan. Khrushchev also appeared from time to time. Molotov was out of
things after his wife's arrest in 1949. He wasn't summoned even during my
father's last illness. Shortly before my father died even some of his intimates
were disgraced: the perennial Vlasik was sent to prison in the winter of 1952
and my father's personal secretary Poskrebyshev,[3] who had been with him for
twenty years, was removed.

access, after all, to more facts than anybody else, but they certainly didn't show it.

As I was leaving, my father called me aside to give me some money. He had started doing this after the war and the currency reform of 1947, when it was no longer the practice to feed and clothe the relatives of Politburo members at state expense. Before that I'd never had money except my stipend at the university and always had to borrow from my "well-to-do" nurse, who earned a fairly good wage.

But after 1947 my father would ask on the rare occasions when we met, "Do you need any money?" Of course I always answered no. "You're only pretending," he'd say. "How much do you need?" I couldn't think what to say. I had no idea what he had in mind, or what length of time the money was supposed to do me for. As for him, he didn't know what the new money was worth or how much anything cost. The only values he knew were the old prerevolutionary ones, whereby a hundred rubles was a munificent sum. So when he handed me two or three thousand rubles without my having the faintest idea what length of time it was for, six months, a month or two weeks, he thought he was giving me a million.

He let his salary pile up in packets every month on his desk. I have no idea whether he had a savings account, but probably not. He never spent any money—he had no place to spend it and nothing to spend it on. Everything he needed—his food, his clothing, his *dachas* and his servants—was paid for by the government. The secret police had a division that existed specially for this purpose and it had a bookkeeping department of its own. God only knows how much it cost and where the money all went. My father certainly didn't know.

Sometimes he'd pounce on his commandants or the generals of his bodyguard, someone like Vlasik, and start cursing: "You parasites! You're making a fortune here. Don't think I

don't know how much money is running through your fingers!"

But the fact was, he knew no such thing. His intuition told
him huge sums were going out the window, but that was all.
From time to time he'd make a stab at auditing the household
accounts, but nothing ever came of it, of course, because the
figures they gave him were faked. He'd be furious, but he
couldn't find out a thing. All-powerful as he was, he was im-
potent in the face of the frightful system that had grown up
around him like a huge honeycomb, and he was helpless
either to destroy it or bring it under control. General Vlasik
laid out millions in my father's name. He spent it on new
houses and trips by enormous special trains, for example. Yet
my father was unable even to get a clear explanation of how
much money was being paid out, where and to whom.

Likewise, he sensed intuitively that I was probably in need
of money. In his later years, when I was a graduate student
at the Academy of Social Sciences, I had a large stipend and
was comparatively well off. But from time to time my father
handed me money anyway with instructions to "give it to
Yasha's daughter."

He did a lot for me that winter. That was the year I divorced
my second husband and left the Zhdanov family. My father
now gave me permission to live in the city rather than the
Kremlin, and I was given the apartment my children and I
live in to this day.

He made only one stipulation, and it was typical of him. All
right, he said. You can live on your own if you like. But then
you can't have a government *dacha* or car any more. "Here's
some money. Go buy a car and drive yourself, but show me
your driver's license first," he said. That suited me fine because
it gave me a certain amount of freedom and a chance to
mingle the way other people did. I could never have borne
living in our old apartment in the Kremlin again.

My father didn't object when I told him I was leaving the Zhdanovs'. "Do as you like," was all he said. Still, he was unhappy about the divorce and didn't like it.

Sometimes he asked me angrily; "What are you, anyway—a parasite, living off what you're given?" When he found out that I paid for my meals and for my apartment he calmed down a bit. He was pleased when I moved into an apartment of my own; he felt I'd been provided for long enough. No one tried harder than he to imbue his children with the idea that they had to support themselves. "Apartments, *dachas,* cars—don't think they're yours. It doesn't any of it belong to you," he said to me again and again.

Now he gave me a packet of money for the last time with the reminder to "give it to Yasha's daughter."

And so I left. I'd intended to come again on Sunday, March 1, but I wasn't able to get through to him on the phone. It was a complicated system. First I had to call his bodyguard. Whoever happened to be on duty would tell me either that "there's movement" or "there's no movement right now." That simply meant my father was asleep or reading quietly in his room, or in any case wasn't stirring around the house. When there was "no movement," it meant I couldn't speak to him on the phone. Since his schedule was so topsy-turvy, he might be asleep no matter what time of day it was.

On the following day, March 2, 1953, I was called out of class at the Academy and told to go to Kuntsevo. But I've told you all that. That's what I started with.

But it's not all. I'm not ready to end my letters yet.

⇥⟫ *19*

Vasily was also summoned on March 2, 1953. He, too, spent several hours sitting in the big room that was so crowded with people. But he was drunk, as he often was by then, and he soon left. He went on drinking and raising Cain in the servants' quarters. He gave the doctors hell and shouted that they had killed or were killing our father. Finally he went home.

He was attending the General Staff Academy at the time. My father had been outraged at Vasily's ignorance and compelled him to go. But my brother no longer was capable of study—he was an alcoholic.

His life was tragic in a way. He was a product and victim of the same system and environment that nurtured and gave rise to the "cult of personality." The system that gave rise to the "cult" also enabled Vasily to make a spectacular career.

212

He started the war as a captain of twenty and finished it as a lieutenant general of twenty-four. He was pushed higher and higher. Those responsible couldn't have cared less about his strengths and weaknesses, any more than they cared what his real abilities were. Their one thought was to curry favor with my father.

Vasily was transferred to Moscow from East Germany in 1947 and promptly made chief of aviation of the Moscow Military District. It was an enormous responsibility. Yet everyone knew he was an alcoholic. He was so ill he could no longer fly his own plane. Nobody seemed to care.

My father saw the state he was in. He scolded him unmercifully. He humiliated him and browbeat him like a little boy in front of everyone, but of course it did no good. Vasily was ill, and what he needed was to be cured. But he didn't want to be cured and nobody dared suggest it. The only authority he cared about was that of my father. He didn't think anyone else was even worth paying attention to. He was surrounded by shady characters from the sports world, masseurs and soccer players, trainers and "promoters," who put him up to all kinds of "deals" such as tampering with hockey and soccer teams and having swimming pools and Palaces of Culture and Sport put up at public expense. As a high-ranking officer of the Military District he had huge sums at his disposal, so lack of money was never any obstacle.

He lived in a big government *dacha*. It had an enormous staff, a stable and kennels, all, of course, at government expense. Everything was permitted him, and he was given anything he wanted. Even Vlasik drank with him and did everything he could to curry favor with him. At the right moment, after all, Vasily could put in a good word for him with my father.

Vasily stopped at nothing. He engaged in intrigue and ex-

ploited his proximity to my father. Anybody who'd fallen out
of favor with him was kicked out of his path and some even
went to jail. No privilege was denied him. He was championed
by even bigger fry than Vlasik—by Beria, Abakumov[1] and
Bulganin, for instance. They twisted him around their little
fingers. They gave him medals, higher and higher rank, horses,
automobiles, privileges, everything. They spoiled and cor-
rupted him, just as long as they needed him. But once my
father was dead and they didn't need him any more, they
abandoned and forgot him.

In 1952 my father himself had had him removed from his
post in the Moscow Military District. It was windy and over-
cast on May Day that year, and the fly-past over Red Square
was canceled. But Vasily went against orders and ordered the
fly-past on his own authority. It was a disaster. The pilots
couldn't stay in formation and very nearly brushed the spires
of the Historical Museum. Several crash-landed. Both pilots
and planes were destroyed.

It was an unheard-of violation of discipline, and one that
had tragic consequences. My father was the one who signed
the order removing Vasily as chief aviation officer of the Moscow Military District.

What on earth were they to do with a lieutenant general
who was unfit for command? My father wanted him to graduate from the General Staff Academy like Artyom Sergeyev,
Vasily's childhood friend with whom he had long since fallen
out. "I'm seventy years old," my father used to say to him,
pointing to the books he was reading on history, literature
and military affairs, "yet I still go on learning."

Vasily agreed to enter the Academy. But he didn't set foot
in the place once. He wasn't capable of it. What he needed
was to be taken to a hospital without a moment's delay and
treated for alcoholism before it was too late. But who was

going to force a general to submit to treatment against his will? To say nothing of its being a general named Stalin.

So he stayed home and drank. It didn't take much. One sip of vodka was enough to make him flop on the sofa and fall asleep.

He remained in this state until the death of our father, which shook him badly. He was convinced that our father had been "poisoned" or "killed." He saw that the world without which he was unable to exist was crumbling all around him, and he was terrified.

Throughout the period before the funeral he was in a dreadful state, and his behavior was appalling. There was no one he didn't blame. He accused the government, the doctors and everybody in sight of using the wrong treatment on our father and failing to give him a proper funeral. He ranted and raved, unmindful of the fact that nobody could get away with behaving that way. He lost any sense of reality or of his own place in the scheme of things and behaved like the crown prince who's just inherited the throne. If anybody had megalomania, it was he.

He was summoned to the Ministry of Defense, and it was suggested that he quiet down. They offered him command of one of the military districts. He refused point-blank. He would take nothing but Moscow and the aviation command of the Moscow Military District. Nothing less would do! They ordered him to a post away from Moscow. Once again he refused. What, they asked, you refuse to accept an order from the Minister of Defense? You don't consider yourself an army officer any more? No, I do not, was his reply. Take off yours stars then, the Minister* concluded in anger.

And so he left the army, a retired general with nothing to do but sit at home and drink.

* The Minister at the time was Bulganin.

He'd thrown his third wife out and persuaded his second wife to come back. By now he was so impossible, however, that even she left. He was completely alone. With neither friends nor a job he was just an alcoholic nobody needed any more.

At this point he lost his head completely. He spent the entire month of April, 1953, going to restaurants and drinking with anyone who happened to be there. He denounced everyone and everything and hadn't the slightest recollection afterward of what he had said. People warned him it might end badly, but he told them all to go to hell. He'd forgotten that things were different now and that he was no longer what he had been once. He was arrested on April 28, 1953, after a drinking bout with foreigners.

Everything came out in the pretrial investigation: the shady deals, the spending, the exploitation of his power and rank beyond any reasonable limit. It came out that he had used his fists on subordinates while on duty. High-level intrigues that had resulted in the arrest of some people and the deaths of others also came to light. Air Force General A. A. Novikov,[2] who had come to grief because of my brother, was released from prison and must have told the story. Everyone and everything was against Vasily now. Not only did no one come forward in his defense, but everyone added fuel to the flames. Everybody gave evidence against him: his former adjutants, aides who'd served under him, generals he hadn't gotten along with, even the Minister of Defense himself. There were enough charges to put ten men in jail.

A military collegium sentenced him to eight years in jail. Vasily couldn't believe it. He bombarded the government with letters—letters of despair, letters admitting all the accusations against him, even threatening letters. He'd lost sight of who he was or where he was and failed to realize that he was a nobody now.

Finally they took pity on him. He was sent to a military hospital in the winter of 1954-55. From there he was supposed to go first to a civilian hospital, then to the Barvikha Sanitarium and finally home. It was Nikita Khrushchev who told me all this. He asked me to come and see him especially in December, 1954, when he was trying to think of a way to help Vasily rehabilitate himself.

Unfortunately, none of it worked. His old friends started coming to the hospital to see him—trainers and athletes, soccer players and various disreputable Georgians. They brought him vodka and he went to pieces again. Forgetting his promises, he resumed his old, rowdy ways. He started threatening people and demanding the impossible all over again.

The result was that he didn't go home from the hospital, but to Vladimir Prison. The sentence of the military collegium was left in effect after all.

In January, 1956, I went to Vladimir[3] to see him. His third wife, Kapitolina, who'd done all she conceivably could to help him, came with me.

I'll remember that excruciating visit as long as I live. We met in the warden's office. A huge portrait of my father left over from the old days was hanging on the wall. The warden was seated at his desk beneath the portrait. Vasily, Kapitolina and I were seated on the sofa opposite. The warden stole a glance at us now and then as we talked. Evidently the wheels were turning slowly in his brain as he struggled to figure out what was going on.

The warden was a short, fair-haired man. The felt boots he was wearing were patched and worn. He had a dark, gloomy office. We sat in front of him, the three of us, Vasily and the two ladies from the capital dressed in expensive fur coats. The warden was in a torment; mental strain was written all over his face.

Vasily told Kapitolina and me to pull every wire we could,

to phone and go to see anyone who'd see us, anything to get him out of there. He made no effort to hide his desperation. He was visibly casting about for someone to turn to, someone he could appeal to. He'd written one member of the government after another, reminding them of the old days and swearing that he'd seen the light and would behave better now.

Kapitolina was a woman of fortitude. She told him not to write letters any more but to be patient and wait a bit. He didn't have too much longer to go. She told him to behave himself, to keep his dignity and be quiet. He just pounced on her. "I ask you for help, and you advise me to be quiet!" Then he turned to me and told me the names of people he thought might help. "It'll be better if you write those people yourself," I said. "Your own word will carry a whole lot more weight than anything I can say."

Later on he wrote me several times telling me to whom I should write and appeal for help. He even thought of getting in touch with the Chinese. "They'll help me," he kept saying, and I suspect that he wasn't far wrong. Kapitolina and I didn't do what he asked us, of course. I knew that no less a person than Khrushchev was doing what he could to help.

Vasily didn't get out of Vladimir until January, 1960. That month Khrushchev called me in again. He was trying to think what to do and how he could help. Someone had thought of suggesting to Vasily that he leave Moscow and go somewhere else to live. The idea was that he ask his wife and family to join him, get a job and change his name.

I told Khrushchev that I didn't think my brother would agree. I did my best to explain that Vasily's alcoholism was a sickness, that he wasn't in control of himself and shouldn't be held responsible for his words and deeds as a person in normal health would be. But I wasn't able to persuade him.

Shortly afterward, Khrushchev summoned Vasily and spent more than an hour with him. Even Vasily said later that Khrushchev had treated him "like a father." They kissed one another on both cheeks and both of them wept. The meeting went well for Vasily. He was to stay in Moscow and was given an apartment on the Frunze Embankment and a *dacha* at Zhukovka near mine. Both his general's rank and his army pension were restored. He was to be allowed to have his own car. He was reinstated as a Communist Party member in good standing. All this was given back to him, all this plus his army medals. The only thing they asked in return was that he get a job and live in peace and try not to be a menace to himself or to anybody else.

They asked one thing more. At the beginning of the conversation Vasily requested that he be allowed to go to Georgia. Khrushchev asked him not to go.

He lived in Moscow for three months, January, February and March. It was no time before he started feeling exactly as he had before. Shady types from Georgia were quick to gather round him. They dragged him to the Aragvi Restaurant and drank with him. They praised him to the skies and glorified him. Once again he started thinking of himself as the crown prince. Nothing could have done him more harm. Did the Georgians want him? By God, he'd go live there then! Could this really be called an apartment, or this stuff furniture? Why, it was an insult to give such furniture to him, of all people! The Georgians would build him a *dacha* near Sukhumi. He'd go there, he would, and live in the style to which he was accustomed. A Georgian woman of uncertain age appeared on the scene, and it was no time at all before she suggested that he marry her and come to live in Sukhumi.

He had a grown son and daughter by this time. They did their best to talk him out of it. His children begged him to get rid of all these hangers-on from Georgia and urged him to turn a deaf ear to their blandishments. They warned him it would end in disaster. He told them that he knew better and that they shouldn't try to tell him what to do.

It did end disastrously, in fact. He was drinking again. He couldn't seem to stay on his feet. His boon companions and above all the Georgians plied him mercilessly with alcohol. In April he finally went to Kislovodsk for "treatment." His daughter, Nadya, went with him. She wrote that his drinking was as bad as ever, that he was indulging in rowdy, even scandalous, behavior, that he was telling everybody where to get off, and that all Kislovodsk was coming to have a look at him. Some crooks drove their cars up from Georgia to take him down with them. He didn't go, but he vanished and after five days reappeared in Kislovodsk, where, it turned out, he'd been living in the house of a switchwoman on the railroad. He returned to Moscow but didn't stay long. By the end of April he had vanished again.

We later found out that he was back serving the same old term in jail, the eight years he'd been serving when he was released and permitted to take up his normal life again. He had now been "requested" to serve out his term since his behavior had been unsatisfactory.

But he wasn't made to finish out his term. He was released in the spring of 1961 from the Lefortovo Prison in Moscow on grounds of ill health. He was suffering from a liver ailment, a stomach ulcer and total debilitation. He had never eaten much, but just filled his stomach with alcohol.

This time he was let out on more stringent conditions than before. He was allowed to live anywhere he liked except Moscow and Georgia. For some reason he chose to go to Kazan. He took along a woman he'd met by chance, a nurse named Masha who worked in the hospital he'd been in. He was given a one-room apartment in Kazan and received his retired general's pension. But he was broken and destroyed both physically and mentally.

He died on March 19, 1962. He'd been on a strenuous drinking bout with some Georgians and never regained consciousness. The autopsy showed that his body had been completely destroyed by alcohol. He was only forty-one years old.

His son and daughter by his first marriage went to the funeral, accompanied by his third wife, Kapitolina. She was the only real friend he had.

Practically the whole city of Kazan turned out for the funeral. They were amazed to see Kapitolina and the children because Masha, the nurse, had succeeded in contracting a bigamous marriage with him and assured everyone that she had been a "faithful friend" to him all her life. She barely allowed the children near the grave.

The cemetery in Kazan now boasts the grave of General V. I. Dzhugashvili and a pretentious inscription by Masha: "To the one and only."

⇛ 20

You're probably worn out by now, my friend, with the countless deaths I've been telling you about. Did I know a single
person whose life turned out well? It was as though my father
were at the center of a black circle and anyone who ventured
inside vanished or perished or was destroyed in one way or
another.

He's been gone for ten years now. Both my aunts, Evgenia
Alliluyeva, Pavel's widow, and Anna Alliluyeva, Redens's
widow and my mother's sister, are back from prison. The
Svanidzes' son, who is my age, is back from exile in Kazakhstan.
Many people have come back, thousands and thousands who
managed somehow to survive. The return of so many people
from prison and exile is a great historic turning point. The
scale on which the dead have come back to life is difficult
to imagine.

In a sense my life, too, couldn't be normal so long as my father was alive. Could I have had as much freedom before as I have now? Could I conceivably have gone any place I wanted to without permission? Could I have met and made friends with anyone I pleased? Could my children have lived freely and without surveillance the way they do now? We can all breathe more freely. It's as though a heavy slab of stone had been lifted from us all. But unfortunately too many things have stayed the same. Russia is too much weighted down by inertia and tradition. The age-old ways of doing things are too strong.

But what is good in Russia is traditional and unchanging, too, even more than what is bad. And perhaps it is this eternal good which gives Russia strength and helps preserve her true self.

My nurse, Alexandra Andreevna, was with me for the first thirty years of my life. If it hadn't been for the even, steady warmth given off by this large and kindly person, I might long ago have gone out of my mind. And after the many losses I have suffered, the death of my nurse, or "Granny," as my children and I used to call her, was my first real loss, the first time I felt I had lost someone really close, someone for whom I had feelings of kinship and love and someone who loved me, too. She died in 1956 after witnessing the return of my aunts from prison and going through the death of my father and grandparents with us. She was more truly a member of the family than anybody else. We celebrated her seventieth birthday a year or so before she died. It was a happy occasion, one that brought all my relatives together, even those who'd been at odds with each other for years. Every one of them loved her and she loved every one of them.

"Granny" was far more than a nurse to me, because she had qualities and talents transcending those of the ordinary nurse even though she'd had no chance to develop them.

Alexandra Andreevna was born on the estate of Maria Behr in the Ryazan district and went to work as a household servant there when she was thirteen years old. Before the Revolution my nurse's entire life was spent with this family and relatives of theirs in St. Petersburg. She worked for them as maid, housekeeper, cook and, finally, as a nurse. She also spent a long time in the household of Nikolai Yevreinov,[1] a well-known theater director and critic, looking after his son. Photographs taken in those years show my nurse as a pretty Petersburg servant. She had a high collar and a topknot on her head. She no longer had anything of the peasant left in her looks.

She was a bright, quick-witted girl, and she learned very fast. As members of the liberal intelligentsia of the period her employers taught her a lot more than how to dress and wear her hair. They taught her to read and helped her discover the world of Russian literature.

She wasn't a sophisticated reader. The heroes of books were living people to her, and it was as though everything written in them had actually taken place. As far as she was concerned, the books she read didn't deal with fictitious events. She never doubted for a moment that Dostoyevsky's *Poor Folk* were real people, the way Gorky's grandmother was.

Gorky once came to see my father at Zubalovo in 1930, while my mother was still alive. When my nurse was caught by Voroshilov sneaking a look into the room through a crack in the door, she told him she "wanted so much to have a peek at Gorky." Voroshilov dragged her into the room. Gorky asked her which of his books she had read and was astonished when she reeled off the titles of practically every one. "Which did you like best?" he asked her. "The story in which you tell how you helped a woman deliver her baby," my nurse replied. And the story called "Birth" was, in fact, her favorite. Gorky was very pleased and shook her hand with real feeling.

She looked back on it with pleasure for the rest of her life and always enjoyed telling about it.

She also saw the poet Demyan Bedny[2] at our house but somehow wasn't enthusiastic about his verse and said only that he was a "bad character."

She lived with the Yevreinovs until the Revolution, when they left for Paris. They were anxious to have her come with them, but she didn't want to leave the country. The younger of her two sons died in one of the famines that swept the countryside during the 1920's. She had to spend several years in her native village, but she couldn't stand the country any more and, as one long accustomed to life in town, no longer had a good word to say about it. She considered the countryside nothing but "mud and filth" and was horrified at the ignorance, superstition and boorishness she'd left behind. She was superb at all kinds of farm work, but had lost interest in it. The land itself held no attraction for her. She wanted, moreover, to give her son a good education, and for that she had to work and earn money in the city.

So she came to Moscow, which she always looked down on. She'd gotten used to St. Petersburg and was permanently spoiled for any other place. (I remember how pleased she was when I went to Leningrad for the first time in 1955. She told me the names of all the streets near her old home and near the bakery she used to go to. She described where she used to sit with the baby carriage and the place on the Neva where she used to buy live fish. I brought back a stack of postcards with pictures of the streets and wide boulevards and the embankment of the Neva River, and we spent a long time looking at them together. She remembered everything and was very much moved. "Moscow's just a village next to Leningrad," she kept saying. "They can keep rebuilding Moscow all they like, but it'll never compare all the same!")

During the 1920's, however, she hadn't any choice but to

live in Moscow, first with the Samarin family and then with the family of a Dr. Malkin. My mother persuaded her to leave the Malkins and come to us.

She came in the spring of 1926, just after I was born. There were three people in the household whom she worshiped. The first was my mother. The second was Bukharin, who was beloved by everyone. He used to spend every summer at our house in Zubalovo with his wife and little girl. Finally, my nurse adored my Grandfather Alliluyev. In my mother's lifetime the spirit of our household was very congenial to her.

"Granny" had had wonderful training in St. Petersburg. She was extremely tactful, she was welcoming and hospitable to anyone who came to the house, she did her work quickly and intelligently, she wasn't unduly curious about her employers' private affairs, and she had equal respect for them all and never gossiped about them or criticized them aloud. She never quarreled with anyone and had an extraordinary capacity to treat everyone with kindness. There was only one person who didn't like her and that was my governess Lidia Georgiyevna, who tried to get her fired and later paid for it. My father thought highly of "Granny" and had nothing but respect for her.

When I was very little she used to read children's stories aloud to me. She had extraordinary talent as a teacher and knew how to turn everything into a game. It was she who taught both me and my children to read. Maybe she'd picked up a lot from the governesses she'd worked with in St. Petersburg. I remember how she taught me to count. She had a lot of little balls of clay of various colors all stuck together. We put them into separate piles, then put them all back together and then we separated them again. That's how she taught me arithmetic even before I had a governess. Later she took me to the preschool music class at the Lomovs' house. Maybe that's where she learned the musical game we used to play. She and I would sit at a table together. She had a good ear and would tap out the rhythm of some song I knew and I'd have to guess what it was. She sang any number of songs to me and she did it with the greatest of gaiety. She knew countless children's stories, folk verses, folk songs and village sayings, and they all came pouring out of her. It was a joy just listening to her.

She had a magnificent command of language. Her Russian was pure, beautiful and with a grammatical perfection rarely heard today. She had a marvelous combination of correct speech—which was, after all, St. Petersburg speech, not that of peasants—and all kinds of bright, sharp-witted sayings. I've no idea where she got them; maybe she made them up herself. For example, I remember her saying not long before she died: "Two lackeys had Mokey—now Mokey's a lackey." She chuckled as she said it.

The old Kremlin, by which I mean the Kremlin of the 1920's and early thirties, was full of people, including children. Whenever she took me out in my carriage, the other children used to gather round and listen spellbound to the stories she had to tell. Eteri Ordzhonikidze, Lyalya Ulyanova, Dodik Menzhinsky—was there one of them my nurse didn't know?

She'd witnessed a good deal in her life. In St. Petersburg she knew not merely the people she worked for but the whole of the circle they moved in. And they were people well known in the arts, people with names like Yevreinov, Trubetskoi, Lanserret, and Musin-Pushkins, the Goerings, van Dervis and others. I showed her a book about the painter Serov[3] once. It was really a book about all the creative intellectuals of St. Petersburg of that day, and she was able to pick out the photographs and names of a great many people she'd been acquainted with. She had countless stories to tell: who used to come to the house and what they wore, how they used to go to the theater to listen to Chaliapin, what they all ate, how their children were brought up, and how they conducted their romances. Both masters and mistresses used to ask her to carry letters to their lovers on the sly.

She'd adopted the Soviet vocabulary and called the ladies she used to work for "bourgeois" women. But there wasn't a hint of malice in the stories she had to tell about them. On the contrary, she thought of her former mistress, Zinaida Yevreinov, with gratitude. It was the same with old Samarin. She knew she'd given them a good deal of herself. But she also knew that they had given a good deal to her, a chance to see and learn a lot.

Later on she came to us, to what was the more or less democratic atmosphere of the Kremlin at that time. In these new surroundings she met a wholly different group of people. They, too, belonged to the so-called upper crust, but their ways of doing things were quite different from anything she'd seen in St. Petersburg. She had marvelous stories to tell about the Kremlin in those days, about Trotsky's "wives" and Bukharin's "wives" and about Clara Zetkin,[4] about the day my father received Ernst Thaelmann[5] in our apartment, about the Menzhinsky[6] sisters and the Dzerzhinsky family. She was a walking chronicle of her age. What a lot she carried with her to the grave!

After my mother's death my nurse was the only stable, unchanging thing left. She was the bulwark of home and family, of what, if it hadn't been for her, would have gone out of my life forever.

Her life had been spent with children and, as a result, she was a bit childlike herself. At all times, no matter what might be going on around her, she was steady, even-tempered and kind. Every day she fed me breakfast and got me off to school in the morning. Every day when I got home from school she saw that I had my dinner. As I was sitting doing my homework she sat in her room, next to mine, doing the things she had to do. At night she put me to bed. It was her kisses and her words I fell asleep to at night ("Little berry, little treasure, little bird") and her kisses I woke up to in the morning ("Get up, little berry, get up, little bird"). I started off each day in her cheery, capable hands.

She lived life with a large and discriminating appetite, with a hunger to see everything, learn everything and experience everything she could.

She was free of bigotry, religious or any other kind. In her youth she had been very religious, but later she ceased observing the rituals and got away from religion as it's observed in the villages, which is a mixture of precepts and prejudices. She kept saying she didn't believe in God any more, but I suspect that she did. I know that before she died she wanted to make a kind of confession to me—that was when she told me about my mother.

Before the Revolution she'd been married and had a family of her own. Then her husband went off to the war, and during the difficult years of the famine he didn't want to come back. In the meantime her younger and favorite son died and she was through for good with the husband who'd left them all alone in the famine-swept countryside. Later on, when her husband found out she was working in the Kremlin, he suddenly remembered her and with true peasant craftiness started bombarding her with letters hinting that he'd like to come back to her. By this time she had a room of her own in Moscow and her elder son was living there.

She had nothing but scorn for her former husband and stood firm. "What do you think of that?" she commented. "I had a hard time for years and I didn't hear a peep out of him. Now he misses me all of a sudden. Let him miss me. I have a son to bring up. I can get along better without him." Her husband made many futile overtures as the years went by, but she never answered. He then trained his two daughters by his second marriage to write her and tell her they were having a hard time and beg for money. She showed me their photographs. They were goggle-eyed, vacant-looking girls. She laughed: "Just look at that. He turned them out like cookies!"

But she felt sorry for them and sent them money regularly, as she did to scores of her own relatives, too. She died with only a few rubles to her name. She didn't save and she didn't put anything by. The way she saw it, you could never do enough for the living.

"Granny" had the greatest tact and consideration, but she also had enormous dignity. One of the things my father liked her for was the fact that there was nothing servile about her. As far as she was concerned everyone was equal. The terms "master" and "mistress" were enough for her. Beyond that it made no difference to her whether her employer was one of the great ones of the earth or not.

No one but the Zhdanovs ever dared call her an "ignorant old woman." I don't think she was ever spoken of so disrespectfully before, not even in the noble families she worked for before the Revolution.

When, during and even before the war, the entire household staff was put on a military footing, "Granny" was officially listed as an employee of the secret police. Before, it was my mother who paid her salary. "Granny" was highly amused to be given the rank of junior sergeant! She saluted the cook whenever she went into the kitchen and said things like "Attention!" or "Aye, aye, sir!" She took the whole business like a nonsensical joke or a game. She didn't want any truck with all these foolish rules. She took care of me and did a good job of

it. She couldn't have cared less what rank they chose to give
her. She'd seen all she wanted of life and witnessed a great
many changes. "First they abolished ranks," she liked to point
out, "and then they brought them back."[7] But as she saw it,
life went on just the same, and it was up to her to do her
job, which in her case was to love children and help people
live no matter what might be going on around them.

Toward the end of her life she was constantly ill. She had
frequent heart spasms and was overweight besides. After she
reached two hundred and twenty pounds, she stopped weighing herself because it only upset her. Even then she kept right
on eating, and as the years went by what had been a healthy
appetite became a compulsion. She could read a cookbook
for hours on end, like a novel, exclaiming as she went along,
"That's how to do it! Right! That's the way we used to make
ice cream at the Samarins'! We put a glass of brandy in, too.
Then we lit it up and when we carried it to the table it was
flaming!" She spent her last two years living with her granddaughter in a little apartment of her own on Plotnikov Street.
Frequently she went walking on Sobachya Ploshchadka. All
the old pensioners of the Arbat gathered there and clustered
round her like members of a club. The whole time she'd be
telling them how she used to make *kulebiaki*[8] and fish pie.
Hearing her talk was enough to make you feel you'd just had
a meal.

It was curiosity that brought on her final illness. One day
at Zubalovo she was looking at television. Suddenly an an-
nouncer came on and said they were about to show the arrival
of the Prime Minister of Burma, U Nu, and that Voroshilov
would meet him at the airport. "Granny" was terribly curious
to see what this U Nu was like and whether Voroshilov had
aged. Forgetting her age, her weight, her heart and her ailing
legs, she started running in from the next room. She stumbled

and fell on the threshold. Her arm was broken and she was very much frightened.

That's how her last illness started. I saw her a week before she died. She asked me to get her a "bit of nice fresh perch." Then I went out of town. On the fourth of February her granddaughter telephoned. Weeping into the phone she told me the news. "Grandmother asked me to open the window. I just turned away for a second. And by the time I turned back, she'd stopped breathing!"

Gripped by a wholly new kind of despair, I quickly went back to Moscow. You'd think I'd have been accustomed to death by this time. But no, I felt as if a piece of my heart had been torn out.

I conferred with her son, and we decided to bury "Granny" next to my mother at Novo-Devichy,* but we had no idea how to go about it. I had the telephone numbers of the heads of various departments in the Moscow City Soviet and the City Party Committee, but I wasn't able to reach them and had no idea how to explain who "Granny" was anyway. Finally I telephoned Voroshilov's wife and told her my nurse had died. They all knew and respected her. Voroshilov himself came to the telephone, sighing and obviously upset. "Of course, of course," he kept saying. "That's the only place to bury her. I'll give the order and it'll be all right."

So we buried my nurse next to my mother after all. "Granny's" nieces and all her relatives were there. Each of us kissed her and wept. I kissed her forehead and hand. I felt no fear or aversion toward death as I did it, only a sense of profound tenderness and melancholy for this being who'd been dearer to me than anyone on earth and was leaving me now as all the others had done.

---

* As Novo-Devichy is considered to be a government cemetery, burial is permitted there only with permission from the higher quarters of the government.

I'm weeping as I write this. Do you see, my dear friend, what "Granny" was to me? I feel the pain of losing her even now. She was like a healthy, sheltering tree of life that rustles its leaves in the sun, that is washed by rain and gleams in the sunlight; that blossomed and bore fruit in spite of all the storms that beat and tried to break it. "Granny" is gone, but the memory of her gaiety and kindness is with me still. My children, too, will never forget how warm and good-natured she was. No one who knew her will ever forget her. Can what is good ever be forgotten?

Don't ever forget what is good in life. Those of our people who have been through the war and the concentration camps (both German and Soviet), who have known prison both under the Czars and in Soviet times, these people who've seen every horror the twentieth century has unleashed on mankind never forget the kindly faces of childhood. Each of them has small, sunny corners he can remember and draw strength from always, through all of life's sufferings. I can only pity anyone who has nothing of this kind to give him solace. Even those who are callous and cruel retain somewhere, hidden from others, such pockets of memory in the depths of their twisted souls.

The Good always wins out. The Good triumphs over everything, though it frequently happens too late—not before the very best people have perished unjustly, senselessly, without rhyme or reason.

*   *   *   *   *

This is how I should like to end my letters to you, my dear friend.

Thank you for your persistence in making me write them. I could never have set in motion this dead weight of memory all by myself. Now that I've managed to shed the intolerable burden that was pressing on me, I feel as though I'd been scaling the cliffs up a mountainside and that at last I've reached the top and can survey the heights which are now far below me. The even mountain ranges stretch out all around me, the rivers are sparkling in the valleys, and the sun is shining over everything. I thank you, my friend.

You've done something else for me, too. You've made me live my life over again. You've given me a chance to see once more those who were near and dear to me even though they've been dead a long time. You've compelled me to wrestle with the difficult and conflicting feelings I've always had for my father—feelings of love and fear, of censure and puzzlement. The past descended on me from all sides all over again and I thought I'd never have the strength to talk to these shadows, these ghosts that came crowding round me.

It was so good to see all of them again. Yet it was terrible at the same time when these dreamlike visions ended. I often wanted to hear their voices some more, but they would suddenly fall silent and disappear.

What sterling, full-blooded people they were, these early knights of the Revolution who carried so much romantic idealism with them to the grave! They were the troubadours, the victims, the blind zealots and the martyrs of the Revolution.

As for those who wanted to set themselves above the Revolution, who wanted to speed up its progress and make tomorrow come today, those who tried to do good by doing evil and make the wheels of time and progress spin faster, have they accomplished what they wanted? Millions were sacrificed senselessly, thousands of talented lives extinguished prematurely. The tale of these losses could not be told in twenty books, never mind twenty letters. Wouldn't it have been better for these people to have gone on serving mankind here on earth rather than have their deaths be the only mark they left in the hearts of men?

History is a stern judge. It's not for me but for history to decide who served the cause of good and who that of vanity and vainglory. I certainly don't have the right.

All I have is my conscience. And conscience tells me that before pointing out the mote in my neighbor's eye I must first see the beam in my own. There's no one, including me, who doesn't have a beam in his own eye.

We are all responsible for everything that happened. Let the judging be done by those who come later, by men and women who didn't know the times and the people we knew. Let it be left to new people to whom these years in Russia will be as remote and inexplicable, as terrible and strange, as the reign of Ivan the Terrible. But I do not think they'll call our era a "progressive" one, or that they'll say it was all for the "good of Russia." Hardly . . .

They will have their say. And what they say will be something new and cogent. Instead of idle whining, they will give voice to a new sense of purpose. They will read through this page in their country's history with a feeling of pain, contrition and bewilderment, and they'll be led by this feeling to live their lives differently.

But I hope they won't forget that what is Good never dies— that it lived on in the hearts of men even in the darkest times and was hidden where no one thought to look for it, that it never died out or disappeared completely.

Everything on our tormented earth that is alive and breathes, that blossoms and bears fruit, lives only by virtue of and in the name of Truth and Good.

Zhukovka
July 16—August 20, 1963

⇒⇒⇒ Translator's Notes

1. GUM: The State Universal Store, largest department store in Moscow, located on Red Square.

2. Yaroslavna: Wife of Prince Igor in the Russian tale "Song of the Host of Igor." When Prince Igor is taken captive, Yaroslavna is left weeping "like a cuckoo" on the fortress wall.

3. "The people are silent": At the end of Pushkin's tragic *Boris Godunov*, the people are called on to proclaim the Pretender Dmitri as Czar. According to Pushkin's final stage instruction for the play, "The people are silent."

1. Georgy Maximilianovich Malenkov, 1902——: Member of Communist Party Central Committee from 1939 and member of Stalin's Politburo from 1946. He assumed the post of Secretary of the Central Committee on Stalin's death but resigned a few days later, March 14, 1953. Chairman of U.S.S.R. Council of

Ministers March 6, 1953—February 9, 1955. Ousted from Central Committee as member of "anti-Party group" in June, 1957.

2. Nikita Sergeyevich Khrushchev, 1894———: First Secretary of the Communist Party Central Committee 1953–64 and Chairman of U.S.S.R. Council of Ministers 1958–64.

3. Nikolai Alexandrovich Bulganin, 1895———: U.S.S.R. Minister of Defense 1947–49, 1953–55. Chairman of U.S.S.R. Council of Ministers from 1955 to 1958, when his association with the so-called "anti-Party group" was made known.

4. Lavrenty Pavlovich Beria, 1899–1953: Held important posts in Cheka and GPU organs in Transcaucasia 1921–31 and was First Secretary of Transcaucasian committee of Communist Party 1932–38. Commissar of Internal Affairs 1938–45 and Deputy Prime Minister in charge of security 1941–53. Arrested in June and shot as an "imperialist agent" in December, 1953.

5. Vladimir Nikitich Vinogradov, 1882–1964: One of nine Kremlin doctors arrested in November, 1952, on charges of conspiring with British and American intelligence services to murder Soviet leaders. They were said to have killed Andrei Zhdanov in 1948. On April 4, 1953, it was announced that the nine accused doctors, plus six others whose arrest had not previously been made public, were released and that the accusation against them had been without legal foundation.

6. Vasily Khrustalyov: Head of Stalin's personal bodyguard.

7. Hall of Columns: A hall in the House of Unions Building, where prominent Soviet personalities lie in state.

8. Kliment Yefremovich Voroshilov, 1881———: Member of Communist Party Central Committee from 1921 and of Politburo from 1926. Appointed Commissar of War and the Navy in 1925; relieved as Commissar of Defense in 1940. Chairman of Presidium of U.S.S.R. Supreme Soviet (titular head of state) 1953–60.

9. Lazar Moiseyevich Kaganovich, 1893———: Member of Communist Party Central Committee from 1924 and of Politburo from 1930. People's Commissar of Transport 1935–44. Deputy Chairman and then First Deputy Chairman U.S.S.R. Council of Ministers 1947–57. Dismissed from office and from Central Committee in June, 1957, as member of "anti-Party group."

10. Anastas Ivanovich Mikoyan, 1895———: Member of Communist Party Central Committee from 1923 and of Politburo from 1935. In charge of foreign and domestic trade from 1926 and of food industries from 1930. Held posts of Deputy Prime Minister and First Deputy Prime Minister during Khrushchev era. Re-

signed as Chairman of Presidium of Supreme Soviet (titular head of state) in December, 1965.

11. Yury Levitan: Well-known Soviet news broadcaster.

LETTER 2, PAGES 15–25

1. Cheka: Abbreviation for the Extraordinary Commission for the Struggle Against Counterrevolution and Sabotage, set up in December, 1917, and later known successively as the GPU, OGPU, NKVD, MVD, MGB, and currently KGB, or State Security Committee. The function of each of these organizations has been maintenance of internal security. Members of the Cheka were known as Chekists.

2. "Mingrelian uprising": Mingrelia is the historical name of the area in western Georgia north of the Rioni River adjacent to the Black Sea which is inhabited by Mingrelians. In 1952 an alleged Mingrelian nationalist organization which included leading local Communist Party officials was liquidated.

3. Ilya Yefimovich Repin, 1844–1929: Russian realist painter.

4. "The sort of warehouse": The property of victims of arrest was confiscated and kept in warehouses until a decision was made as to its disposal.

5. Leninskiye Gorki: Lenin's country residence outside Moscow, where he died.

6. Twentieth Congress: The Twentieth Congress of the Soviet Communist Party of February, 1956, at which Khrushchev delivered the "secret speech" denouncing Stalin.

LETTER 3, PAGES 26–36

1. Boris Mikhailovich Shaposhnikov, 1882–1945: Marshal of the Soviet Union. Chief of Staff of Red Army and Deputy People's Commissar of Defense in 1930's. Chief of Staff again in 1941–42; appointed head of Voroshilov Military Academy 1943.

2. Ivan Andreyevich Krylov, 1769–1844: Russian writer and fabulist.

3. Nikolai Ivanovich Bukharin, 1888–1938: A leading Communist Party theoretician. During the 1920's supported Stalin against Trotsky and later against Zinoviev and Kamenev. He favored continuation of the New Economic Policy, however, and in 1928–29 he was, together with Rykov and Tomsky, leader of the so-called Right Opposition to Stalin. In spite of this he remained a member of the Central Committee until 1936 and took an active part in drawing up the 1936 Constitution. In March,

1937, he was accused of being a "Trotskyite" and expelled from the Party. In March, 1938, in the last great "show" trial of the purges, he was found guilty of treason and executed.

4. Grigory Konstantinovich Ordzhonikidze, 1886–1936: Became a Bolshevik in 1903 and was active in Georgian revolutionary movement. Directed the Communist Party in the Caucasus in 1920 and in Transcaucasia 1921–26. Became Politburo member and Chairman of Supreme Council of National Economy in 1930 and Commissar of Heavy Industry in 1932. Sided with Stalin against Trotsky during 1920's but is thought to have tried to limit scope of purges. His death was discussed by Khrushchev at Twentieth Party Congress in 1956.

5. Semyon Mikhailovich Budyonny, 1883——: Commander of First Cavalry Army during Russian Civil War and Marshal of Soviet Union from 1935.

6. Sochi: Soviet resort on Black Sea coast of Abkhazia, in the Caucasus.

7. Abel Sofronovich Yenukidze, 1877–1937: Joined revolutionary movement in the Caucasus in 1890's and became member of Communist Party Central Committee after the Revolution. Disappeared during purges of 1930's.

8. Vyacheslav Mikhailovich Molotov, 1890——: Commissar (later Minister) of Foreign Affairs 1939–49 and 1953–56. Dismissed in 1957 as member of Central Committee and First Deputy Prime Minister as member of "anti-Party group."

9. Gorodki: A game resembling skittles.

10. Felix Edmundovich Dzerzhinsky, 1877–1926: A Soviet leader of Polish origin, elected to Bolshevik Central Committee in August, 1917, who took active part in preparation of October Revolution. Nominated by Lenin in December, 1917, to be first head of Cheka (from 1922 known as OGPU) and held this post until his death in 1926.

LETTER 4, PAGES 37–51

1. Tiflis: Prerevolutionary name for Tbilisi, now capital of Soviet republic of Georgia.

2. Mikhail Ivanovich Kalinin, 1875–1946: Titular head of Soviet state from March, 1919, until his death in 1946. A popular figure who was said frequently to help in hardship cases and was known as "Papa" Kalinin.

3. Ivan Timofeyevich Fioletov, 1844–1918: Member of Com-

munist Party from 1900 and early participant in revolutionary movement. Shot by the British in Baku in September, 1918.

4. Shatura: A power station between Moscow and Leningrad, construction of which was one of the major electrification projects of the 1920's.

5. Zinovy Yakovlevich Litvin-Sedoi, 1876–1947: Communist Party member from 1897. A leader of December, 1905, uprising in Moscow and participant in Russian Civil War.

6. War Communism: The name by which the social and economic policy of the Soviet Government from 1918 to 1921 is known. A period of nationalization of industry and trade, wages in kind for workers and employees, compulsory food delivery by peasants and obligatory labor service by the middle classes. A rigorous period ended by the so-called strategic retreat of the New Economic Policy.

LETTER 5, PAGES 52–66

1. Nikolai Nikolayevich Urvantsev, 1893——: Arctic explorer and geologist, who explored the Taimyr Peninsula in northern Siberia after 1919; Deputy Director of the Arctic Institute in Leningrad, 1932–38.

2. People's Commissariat of Defense: Later renamed Ministry of Defense.

3. Sergei Mironovich Kirov, 1886–1934: Helped establish Soviet power in Caucasus after 1917. Head of Communist Party in Azerbaidzhan from 1921 and in Leningrad from 1926. Became member of Politburo in 1930. Supported Stalin against his rivals but is thought to have led opposition to Stalin's personal rule following Seventeenth Party Congress in 1934. His assassination by a young Party member called Nikolayev in 1934 started the terror that developed into the purges.

4. Pyotr Nikolayevich Fedoseyev, 1908——: Communist Party philosopher who worked for Central Committee 1941–47, was chief editor of Party theoretical journal *Bolshevik* 1946–49 and was subsequently editor of the journals *Party Life* and *Problems of Philosophy*. Director of the Institute of Philosophy, U.S.S.R. Academy of Sciences, 1955–62.

5. Lina Solomonovna Shtern, 1878——: Distinguished physiologist, graduate of Geneva University, who came to U.S.S.R. from Latvia in 1925. Professor of Second Medical Institute and director of Institute of Physiology 1925–49. Linked with "doctors' plot" in 1953. Associated with Institute of Biological Physics, U.S.S.R. Academy of Sciences, since 1954.

6. Solomon Abramovich Lozovsky, 1878–1952: Bolshevik trade union leader who emigrated in 1909 and returned in 1917. Was Secretary General of Profintern (Communist trade union international) and was also active in Comintern. Served as Vice Commissar of Foreign Affairs and became assistant director of Soviet Information Bureau after 1944. Purged in 1949 in connection with "anticosmopolitan" campaign. Rehabilitation announced in 1956.

7. Polina Semyonovna (Zhemchuzhina) Molotov, 1896——: Named head of Perfume Trust in 1932 and Commissar of Fish Industries in 1939.

8. "Permit to stay in Moscow": To live in the city it is necessary to have a residence permit stamped in one's internal passport by the local militia. It is difficult to obtain a residence permit for Moscow and some other large cities because of crowded housing conditions.

9. Kamo (Semyon Arshakovich Ter-Petrosyan), 1882–1922: Bolshevik from 1903 and "expropriator" who was frequently arrested and escaped. Under Stalin's supervision organized bank robberies in Tiflis and Kutaisi in 1907 and was sentenced to death four times prior to Revolution. After 1917 worked with Cheka and in Red Army. Died in an auto accident.

LETTER 7, PAGES 73–82

1. Jan Borisovich Gamarnik, 1894–1937: Bolshevik military leader who was head of political administration of Red Army. Member of Central Committee 1927–34. Committed suicide in May, 1937, apparently to avoid arrest and trial for treason. Posthumously rehabilitated at Twentieth Party Congress in 1956.

2. John Reed, 1887–1920: American journalist who went to Russia in 1917. Author of *Ten Days That Shook the World*, eyewitness account of October, 1917, Revolution. Buried in Kremlin wall.

3. Nikolai Ivanovich Yezhov, 1894?–1939?: Member of Party Central Committee from 1934 and Secretary of Central Committee from 1935. In 1936 was appointed chief of NKVD, or secret police, and for two years directed the purges, which were known as the "Yezhovshchina." Succeeded in 1938 by Beria and disappeared in 1939.

4. Twenty-second Party Congress: October, 1961.

5. Ukhta: Center of prison camp complex in Komi Autonomous Republic.

LETTER 8, PAGES 83-94

1. Ivan Ivanovich Radchenko, 1874–1942: Communist Party member from 1898 and active in revolutionary movement in St. Petersburg. Organized Chief Administration of Fuel Industry at Lenin's request in 1918, active in fuel industry until 1937.

2. "I had a lot of threes": The marking system in secondary schools during prerevolutionary times was similar to that of the present day—on a scale of one to five, with five being the highest mark, or "excellent."

3. Nikolai Semyonovich Chkheidze, 1864–1926: Menshevik leader in Third and Fourth Dumas, First Chairman of Petrograd Soviet after February Revolution in 1917. In 1918 went to Georgia and was elected Chairman of Constituent Assembly. In 1921, after conquest of Georgia by Bolsheviks, he emigrated. Committed suicide in 1926.

4. Field of Mars: A square in Leningrad where workers and peasants who died during Revolution of February, 1917, were buried.

5. Leonid Borisovich Krasin, 1870–1926: Engineer and diplomat who took part in Brest-Litovsk peace negotiations and in March, 1921, signed first Anglo-Soviet agreement. Took part in Genoa and Hague International Conferences in 1922. Appointed Soviet Ambassador to France in 1924 and to London in 1925. Died in London.

6. Lidia Alexandrovna Fotiyeva, 1881——: Private secretary to Lenin, 1918–24.

LETTER 9, PAGES 95–110

1. Arbat: A major thoroughfare in Moscow.

2. Max and Moritz: A German children's book by Wilhelm Busch, 1832–1908, well-known German humorist and children's writer.

3. Andrei Andreyevich Andreyev, 1895——: Member of Politburo 1932–52; Secretary of Communist Party Central Committee 1935–46; Commissar of Agriculture 1943–46; Vice Chairman U.S.S.R. Council of Ministers 1946–53.

4. Maxim Maximovich Litvinov, 1876–1951: People's Commissar of Foreign Affairs 1930–39 and Soviet Ambassador to United States 1941–43. Deputy Foreign Minister of U.S.S.R. until 1946.

LETTER 12, PAGES 121–141

1. "Some celebrated meetings": In July, 1956, and the summer of 1960.

2. "Repressed": The word for "liquidate." Could mean being sent to camps or prisons or being shot.

3. Dmitri Dmitriyevich Pletnyov, 1872–19?: Doctor found guilty at trial of Bukharin and Rykov in March, 1938, of complicity in deaths of Gorky and Kuibyshev and sentenced to twenty-five years' imprisonment.

4. Lev Grigoryevich Levin, 1870–1938: Doctor sentenced to death at trial of Bukharin and Rykov in March, 1938, for allegedly killing Gorky and Kuibyshev and for complicity in death of Menzhinsky.

5. Robert Indrikovich Eikhe, 1890–1940: Central Committee member of Latvian origin, shot in 1940 for alleged opposition activities. In "secret speech" of February, 1956, Khrushchev said the case against Eikhe had been fabricated.

LETTER 13, PAGES 142–156

1. Pioneers: Soviet children's organization.

2. Ritsa: A mountain lake near Sochi.

3. "Housekeeper" or "Mistress": The Russian word is "Khozyaika," feminine for "Khozyain" or "Master," as Stalin was known to those around him.

LETTER 15, PAGES 164–172

1. Acmeists: A school of poetry founded by Nikolai Gumilov in 1913 as a reaction against symbolism.

LETTER 16, PAGES 173–183

1. Roman Lazarevich Karmen, 1906——: Well-known film director.

2. Konstantin Mikhailovich Simonov, 1915——: Soviet poet, playwright and novelist. Achieved great popularity during war with his war dispatches, patriotic poems and novel on siege of Stalingrad, Days and Nights, published in 1945.

3. Anna Akhmatova, 1886–1966: Russian poet.

4. Nikolai Stepanovich Gumilov, 1886–1921: Russian poet who was executed for alleged participation in conspiracy against Soviet Government.

5. Vladislav Felitzianovich Khodasevich, 1886–1939: Russian poet and literary critic who died in Paris.

6. Vorkuta: Town in Pechora basin coal mining center in Komi Autonomous Republic. Site of prison camp complex.

7. Inta: Another town in Pechora basin coal mining center in Komi Autonomous Republic. Many prisoners were sent there to work.

LETTER 17, PAGES 184–204

1. "Minister of Defense": During the war Stalin took the title Minister of Defense as well as that of Prime Minister.

2. Andrei Alexandrovich Zhdanov, 1896–1948: Head of Leningrad Party organization 1934–44, member of Politburo from 1939. As Secretary of Central Committee in charge of ideology, he directed the postwar campaigns against "formalism" and Western influences in the arts and against "objectivism" in scholarship. Also played leading role in campaign against "cosmopolitanism." Thought to have been Stalin's heir apparent when he died of heart attack.

3. Solomon Mikhailovich Mikhoels, 1890–1948: Outstanding Jewish actor and director; artistic director of State Yiddish Theater in Moscow from 1929 until closing of theater in 1948 during campaign against "cosmopolitanism." Died in mysterious circumstances a few months later.

4. "What he'd gotten himself into": Soon after his appointment to the Science Section of the Central Committee, Zhdanov made a speech criticizing Lysenko. On August 7, 1948, *Pravda* published a letter from Yury Zhdanov to Stalin apologizing for this "mistake" caused by "inexperience and immaturity."

LETTER 18, PAGES 205–211

1. "Presents": Gifts were sent to Stalin from all over the world in honor of his seventieth birthday in December, 1949.

2. Lidia Timashuk: Obscure woman medical worker who wrote a letter to Stalin in late 1952 denouncing nine doctors in the "case of the Kremlin doctors." On January 20, 1953, Dr. Timashuk was awarded the Order of Lenin for her denunciation. On April 4, 1953, when release of the doctors was announced, *Pravda* also announced that the Order of Lenin awarded Dr. Timashuk had been revoked.

3. Alexander N. Poskrebyshev, 1891–1966: A Party member from

1917 who went to work in Party Secretariat in 1922 or 1923. From early 1930's was part of Stalin's personal secretariat.

1. Viktor S. Abakumov, 1897?–1954?: Worked in Cheka in Ukraine 1920–22, later head of OGPU in Urals and western Siberia. Head of counterespionage organization SMERSH during the war. Minister of State Security 1946–51. Tried for treason in December, 1954, and executed.

2. Alexander Alexandrovich Novikov, 1900——: Chief of aviation on Leningrad front during World War II. Chief Air Marshal of Soviet Union and Vice Commissar of Defense 1942–1946. Fell into disfavor soon after the war. Named Deputy Chief Air Marshal of Soviet Union in 1954 and head of Higher Aviation Academy in 1956.

3. Vladimir: Town 110 miles northeast of Moscow where prison is located.

1. Nikolai Nikolayevich Yevreinov, 1879–1953: Theater director and playwright who opposed Moscow Art Theater method, was a master of stylized spectacle and held aesthetic views close to those of Oscar Wilde. Emigrated in 1920's and produced plays in Europe and America.

2. Demyan Bedny, 1883–1945: "Proletarian" poet of Soviet period.

3. Valentin Alexandrovich Serov, 1865–1922: Russian painter.

4. Clara Zetkin, 1857–1933: One of the founders of German Communist Party and of the Comintern. Lived in U.S.S.R. 1923–1927.

5. Ernst Thaelmann, 1886–1944: Head of Communist Party of Germany before the rise of Hitler.

6. Vyacheslav Rudolfovich Menzhinsky, 1874–1934: Deputy head of OGPU in 1923; became second head of OGPU in 1926, succeeding Dzherzhinsky.

7. "First they abolished ranks": Ranks for officers of Red Army and other organizations were abolished after 1917 Revolution and reintroduced during the Second World War.

8. *Kulebiaki*: Pastry made with meat, fish or cabbage.